# Managing Challenging Children

**Dedication**

To Debbie, Clint and Anne-Marie; my loves, my strength, my inspiration.


**Acknowledgement**

To Chris, whose support, trust and friendship made this book possible.

**About The Author**

Gerard Gordon is the founder and Training Director of *Managing Challenging Children*, an Australian-based educational consultancy.

Since graduating as a teacher in 1979 he has worked in a variety of educational settings, including withdrawal centres for children with social, emotional and behavioural problems.

In 1990 he began work as a member of an 'outreach' support team for schools with difficult-to-manage children, where he became interested in teacher development. In 1994 he left teaching to become a full-time professional development provider in the United Kingdom. Gerard has since been working in schools, developing resources for teachers and speaking about classroom management both in Australia and the United Kingdom.

# Managing Challenging Children

**Gerard Gordon**

Managing Challenging Children

ISBN 1 86400 302 2


First Published in 1996

by Prim-Ed Publishing


Australia

P.O. Box 332 Greenwood Western Australia 6024

United Kingdom

P.O. Box 051, Nuneaton, CV11 6ZU

Republic of Ireland

P.O. Box 8, New Ross, Co. Wexford

# Contents

'If no-one out there
understands,
start your own
revolution and cut out
the middle man.
In a perfect world we'd
all sing in tune,
but this is reality so give
me some room.
So join the struggle
while you may,
the revolution is just a
T-shirt away.

Waiting for the great
leap forward.'

...B. Bragg.

Hanging over the entrance of every teacher training institution there should be a large sign that says:

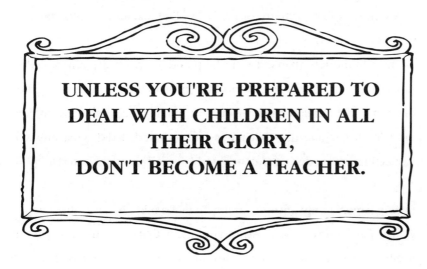

**UNLESS YOU'RE PREPARED TO DEAL WITH CHILDREN IN ALL THEIR GLORY, DON'T BECOME A TEACHER.**

Prospective teachers should know that children will *always* test the limits. They should know children will invariably talk out of turn, run rather than walk, daydream rather than listen, test your authority rather than acquiesce meekly… and generally question your every utterance.

Prospective teachers need to know that the way they deal with this naturally explorative childish behaviour can either make or break them. Effective behaviour management can mean the difference between a long and satisfying career, or a life of constant stress and worry leading to early retirement — or possibly worse!

I didn't have the benefit of that sign hanging over the doors at the institution where I trained and as a new graduate I realised the units I had studied at college in no way prepared me for the gritty reality that is the classroom. In hindsight, the qualities that got me through those difficult first years were a boundless enthusiasm and, more importantly, an understanding mentor whose shoulder was often the only warm, secure, comforting place I could find in the entire school.

More by good luck than by good management I survived my 'Baptism of Fire'. I emerged shell-shocked but acutely aware that classroom teaching is one of the most difficult jobs available in the work force. Having to be responsible for one or two children is difficult enough. Being responsible for thirty or more can be amazingly demanding.

Eventually though, thanks to the help and support of many people, I moved beyond 'survival mode' and began searching for ways to make a difference to the children in my care. Surrounding me were many different models of teaching my colleagues had adopted. I did what any self-respecting novice does: I watched and I copied what appeared to work.

**I watched and I copied what appeared to work.**

Owing largely to my uncanny ability to make mistakes, my effectiveness as a teacher grew slowly. An environment that once used to present itself as a maelstrom of chaotic, disconnected and unpredictable events soon began to form itself into a fairly consistent pattern of processes I could understand and work with: I was becoming a real teacher! I recall with surprising clarity the shock and amusement I felt the first time a beginning teacher asked ME for advice.

Possessed of a new-found confidence I decided to specialise and applied for a job working at a purpose-built centre for children with social, behavioural and/or emotional 'problems'. Once again, my safe little world was turned upside down and I found myself thrust into an environment where confusion and 'unpredictability' were again the norm. However, owing to the fact that I happen to be blessed with an iron constitution and a will to survive, I eventually began to learn new patterns of behaviour management from my more experienced colleagues.

Willing I was, skilful I wasn't, yet through sheer **tenacity** it came to pass that I found myself the most experienced member on staff.

It was just at this time when, with snail-like speed, I seemed to have mastered a small repertoire of management skills, that **it happened.**

The centre for emotionally and behaviourally disturbed children changed its model from one of withdrawal to one of outreach. No longer would children be withdrawn to a special place to be 'fixed' before returning to their regular classes. Now we would go directly to them. My role became one of providing training and support for teachers and schools who had 'difficult-to-manage children'. I would be helping them to help their children.

**No longer would children be withdrawn to a special place to be 'fixed' before returning to their regular classes.**

This service shift turned out to have an incredibly powerful effect on my professional and personal life. The opportunity to work in literally hundreds of classrooms meant I was exposed to models of teaching excellence I had previously never dreamed possible. There were, it seemed to me, teachers working in classrooms who were a quantum leap ahead of me in terms of their effectiveness in managing challenging behaviour.

I have been in awe on many occasions, left marvelling at the finely honed craft that managing challenging behaviour is. Recognising the opportunity with which I had been presented, I observed, took notes, asked questions, videotaped, confronted and at times 'apprenticed' myself to these wizards.

This book is the culmination of those years spent 'marvelling and modelling'. It's an attempt to hold up for scrutiny those belief systems, understandings, notions, ideas, strategies and techniques that can make a profound difference to the way a classroom runs.

Sadly, not every graduate is fortunate enough to be 'mentored' in the skills of managing challenging children, but perhaps this book can help in some small way.

Reality is *a shared belief system about the world and the way it works.* This book is the reality that I share with some truly remarkable teachers. Take from it those things that work for you.

**Take from it those things that work for you.**

# CHAPTER 1

# The Effect of Belief Systems in the Classroom

Whether we realise it or not, we each carry around with us a mental blueprint or picture of ourselves. It may be ill-defined and vague to our conscious gaze. In fact, it may not be recognisable consciously at all. But it is there, complete down to the last detail. This self-image is our own understanding of 'the sort of person I am'. It has been built up of 'beliefs' about ourselves. Once an idea becomes a part of this 'self', it becomes true as far as we are personally concerned. We do not question its validity, but we proceed to act upon it, *as if* it were true. Our belief systems are massive generalisations we make about life. They are our own personal set of rules about ourselves and what we are capable of, about the world and the way it works and about other people and how they behave. A belief system is simply an *internal* model we create to represent our world. One of the most powerful conceptual ideas put forward by psychologists in recent years is the *self-fulfilling prophecy*, the notion that your beliefs tend to act like an automatic guidance system on the direction of your life. Whatever your belief system is about the world, you will find the world tends to live up or down to your expectations.

The first thing that struck me about the exceptional teachers I was working with was they all seemed to share a common belief system. Effective teachers, it seems, achieve success with difficult children *primarily* because they **believe that they can.** Deeply embedded within their central nervous systems is their deep conviction that...difficult doesn't mean impossible.

**...difficult doesn't mean impossible.**

**Effective teachers don't expect miracles, they rely on them.**

This empowering belief system drives them, like a powerful motor, towards success. Effective teachers, it seems, have a central nervous system that is wired up in such a way that no other outcome besides success is possible. Whether these teachers know it or not, the world, and the children in it, live up to their empowering expectations. Effective teachers don't expect miracles, they rely on them.

Struggling for ways to describe how this empowering belief system affects the behaviour of teachers who make a difference, I stumbled upon the term **'AS IF'**. This term seemed perfect: it struck an immediate chord of recognition in me.

Highly successful teachers choose to behave **as if** they make a difference. They act **as if** a difficult child is already behaving appropriately. They smile at a difficult child **as if** he or she were a valued member of the classroom. They speak to the child **as if** the child were listening carefully. They approach the child **as if** the child will appreciate their presence.

Even when things appear to be going manifestly wrong, effective teachers continue to act **as if** things are actually going well. It's **as if** their psyches have closed down to the possibility of failure. This **as if** strategy is a premise upon which effective teachers base their behaviour, their personality, and even their circumstances. Because of this, their experience seems to verify and thereby strengthen their belief system, and a beneficial cycle is set up.

## The Empowering Model

As a result of their empowering belief system, some teachers set up a very powerful set of circumstances that creates an invisible structural necessity for children to live up to this self-fulfilling prophecy of success.

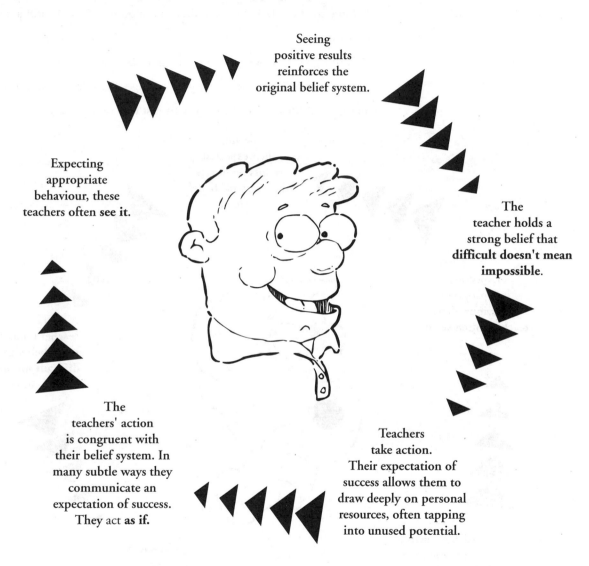

Seeing
positive results
reinforces the
original belief system.

Expecting
appropriate
behaviour, these
teachers often **see it**.

The
teacher holds a
strong belief that
**difficult doesn't mean
impossible**.

The
teachers' action
is congruent with
their belief system. In
many subtle ways they
communicate an
expectation of success.
They act **as if**.

Teachers
take action.
Their expectation of
success allows them to
draw deeply on personal
resources, often tapping
into unused potential.

## The 'Disempowering' Model

Our belief system about the way the universe operates sends a direct signal to our nervous system and causes us to filter what we see as real. Holding this filtered reality as truth, we behave in ways that tend to reinforce the very belief system that operated to affect our behaviour in the first place.

If I could give just one gift to every graduate teacher it would be this empowering belief in their ability to manage challenging children. Oh, what great things could happen with just this one small gift.

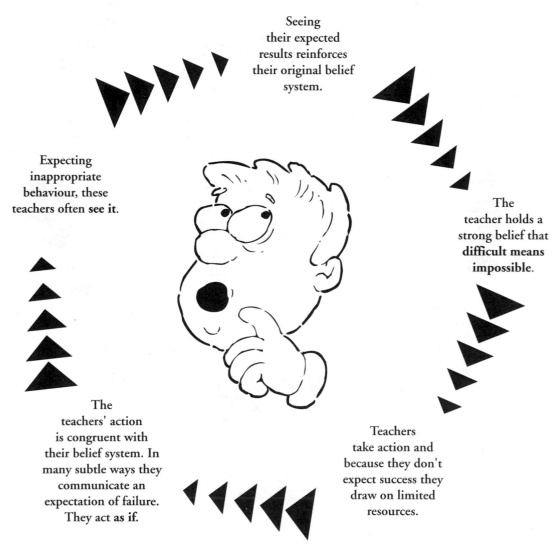

Seeing their expected results reinforces their original belief system.

Expecting inappropriate behaviour, these teachers often **see it**.

The teacher holds a strong belief that **difficult means impossible**.

The teachers' action is congruent with their belief system. In many subtle ways they communicate an expectation of failure. They act **as if**.

Teachers take action and because they don't expect success they draw on limited resources.

Human beings form the massive generalisations that we call a belief system as young children. Far from being *informed, conscious, adult choices,* our belief systems are created as children through interacting with countless influences. These include parents, teachers, peers and television. Unfortunately, once these internal models are formed, most people will go to extraordinary lengths to defend what they believe to be true. It is lucky for the human race our beliefs are not part of our genetic code and that we do in fact make them up. Have you 'made up' a belief system about managing challenging children? Does it operate to increase or lessen your likelihood of success in the classroom? Do you want to change this belief system? Great, because the good news is — you can change at any time you choose! All you need is commitment and a little bit of know-how. The notion is this: because belief systems are generalisations we make up about the world before we are fully informed decision makers, we can, as informed adults, change our belief systems to ones that will empower us instead of limit us.

**...our belief systems are created as children through interacting with countless influences.**

Imagine, if you will, that a belief system is a giant creature that, because of its size, is supported by many legs. Just as the easiest way to bring down the giant creature is to weaken its smaller legs, so the easiest way to bring down a 'disempowering' belief system is to attack the smaller assumptions upon which it stands. These smaller assumptions are generally intertwined and, discovering the fallacy of one or two of them can actually lead to a domino effect that is powerful enough to bring an entire belief system crashing down.

**...we can, as informed adults, change our belief systems to ones that will empower us instead of limit us.**

The chapter on *Perception* (Chapter 2) and the chapter on *Assumptions About Behaviour* (Chapter 3) have been written with this goal specifically in mind. They will help you examine the smaller assumptions upon which an empowering belief system about managing challenging behaviour rests. Scrutinising them carefully may assist you to create a 'success cycle' in your classroom.

However, by far the easiest way I've found to change a belief system is to simply act **as if** it has changed.

When teachers say to me, *Gerry, I understand what you are saying about belief systems but I've had mine too long and I can't change,* I respond sympathetically and say, *Of course you can't change, I realise that it would be much too hard in your particular case, so why don't we just pretend you've changed instead. Now what sort of things might you do?*

For all its amazing power, it seems your brain can't tell the difference between managing challenging children with an empowering belief system and managing challenging children while PRETENDING to have an empowering belief system. In the end, the results are the same. You act **as if** and your brain is 'tricked' into a success cycle.

Of course, the real pay-off is that the children in your classroom are swept up by your cycle of success. By acting **as if**, whether pretending or not, you will create an invisible structural need for the children to live up to your expectations of them.

After every Olympic Games the gold medal winners are interviewed by members of the press. When asked about the reason for their success, champion after champion replies, 'I couldn't have achieved what I have achieved without my_____ (Mum, Dad, husband, wife, friend, coach) who never stopped believing in me'.

Be the person who changes lives. Be the person who never stops believing.

**Be the person who changes lives.**

For everybody's sake EXPECT THE BEST, because when you do, you very often get it!

## SUMMARY

- Your beliefs about challenging behaviour affect the way you deal with it.
- Negative or positive behaviour will exist in your class as a direct result of your belief systems.
- You can change your belief system at any time you wish.
- Effective teachers create beneficial cycles in their classrooms by acting **as if**.

# CHAPTER 2

## Focus — The Power of Perception

...'Instead of saying, "If I hadn't seen it I wouldn't have believed it," we should be saying, "If I hadn't believed it with all my heart I wouldn't have seen it." '...

...Edward DeBono.

The voice at the other end of the phone was strained, and even with my stunted sensitivity I detected a sense of urgency in the hurried words of the deputy principal.

*Gerry, morning recess and lunch break are a nightmare at our school. The detention rooms are full, the teachers are at their wits' end and things seem to be getting worse. We'd appreciate any input you'd be able to give us.*

*Sure,* I replied in my best self-assured manner, *let's make an appointment for lunchtime tomorrow.*

The drive the following lunchtime was made in brilliant spring sunshine and after a few niceties with the administration team I sallied forth into the great unknown that is the playground. Ready to flee for my life at any moment, coiled like a nervous springbok at a crowded watering hole, I made my way tentatively around the generously shaded oval. Ten minutes passed and there were no signs of bruising on my body, or anybody else's for that matter. In fact, I was having a lovely time!

I actually found the children to be very pleasant indeed. I saw cooperative groups at play. I saw the mutual sharing of equipment. I saw sensitive exchanges and a basic 'fun and frolic' attitude among the children. I also saw other displays of childish behaviour: running instead of walking, arguing over points of order and a general testing of adult-imposed boundaries. Everything appeared quite normal to me. In fact, because I had previously been working in what for me was a particularly explosive and demanding playground, my perception of the situation was quite different from the deputy's.

**Everything appeared quite normal to me.**

From past experience I've learned you can't change the way a person 'sees' a situation just by telling him/her you 'see' it differently. What you can do, on the other hand, is partially match the person's view but give him/her a tool for 'seeing' things differently. This way you can usually 'reframe' the problem and cause the person to have a focus change.

**...give him/her a tool for 'seeing' things differently.**

With this strategy in mind, I didn't return to the deputy's office and try to convince him that he and his staff didn't really have a difficult problem. It would have been pointless for me to tell him that if he changed his perspective he'd actually find the playground a very pleasant place indeed.

Attempting to 'reframe' the problem I returned to the deputy's office and said, *I can really see the problems that you're having. Something ought to be done straight away and I have a proposed action plan for you. What I want you and your staff to do is to put away those red tokens that you give out every time you see someone behaving badly, and give out these gold tokens every time you see someone behaving well.*

I went on to explain that for the scheme to work effectively the staff would have to give out as many tokens for 'good' behaviour as they possibly could, even for the smallest possible 'good' thing.

Then I left.

Two weeks later I received a phone call from the same deputy.

*Gerry, you're a miracle worker. The entire atmosphere in the playground is different. Within two weeks of following your advice the staff have managed to completely change the children's behaviour.*

**This I had to see.** I'd hardly had time to park the car before I'd realised what had changed about the children's behaviour.

**Practically nothing!** These were the same children doing the same things in the same setting. What had changed was the teacher's PERSPECTIVE. Instead of looking for 'bad' behaviour and giving out red tokens, they were now looking for 'good' behaviour and giving out gold tokens and, what it is you LOOK for, you very often SEE!

**...what it is you look for, you very often see!**

**Put very simply — you can make a difference!**

There are elements in the way behaviour is viewed at the school level that either amplify or decrease its significance. Put very simply - you can make a difference!

As teachers we have to remember that what we observe is not nature itself, but nature exposed to our methods of processing information. In other words, we do not **get** meanings from our environment, we **create** them.

Human perception works very much like a cameras focus. When you point a camera and focus it on a subject you automatically ignore most of the available background material. The snapshot you take is at the expense of all you have ignored. When you point your perception at a subject you automatically delete most of the available background material. What you perceive is at the expense of all you have left out. All of us have choices in life. We can choose our focus. We can choose to adopt a negative or a positive view of the world. We can consciously look for positive empowering situations, *because what it is we look for we very often find,* or we can let our focus wander and many times settle into a negative view. If we don't consciously monitor our focus it **will** wander and settle where it will. If we don't have a target we don't have anything to aim for.

All the talented teachers I've had the pleasure of working with use a strategy that can best be described as a conscious effort to **control their own focus.** They deliberately look for what it is they hope to find: **appropriate behaviour.**

**...look for what it is they hope to find:**

## The Greens and Sandtraps Strategy

Successful golfers need to know where the greens and the sandtraps are. However, they don't focus continually on the sandtraps, where they don't want to go. Instead, they let their mind focus and settle on the greens.

Highly gifted managers of challenging behaviour take the following steps to control their focus and create a positive view in their classroom.

1. **Give an instruction.**
   ▼
2. **Give 'wait time'.**
   ▼
3. **Look for appropriate behaviour.**
   ▼
4. **Acknowledge appropriate behaviour.**

### Step 1. Give an instruction.

When accomplished teachers give an instruction to children they communicate a positive expectation of compliance. The way these teachers stand, use their voices and eye contact lets children know that they expect appropriate behaviour. In many subtle but observable ways their actions are congruent with their empowering belief system. They act **as if**!

### Step 2. Give 'wait time'...

Successful teachers don't seem to be doing anything immediately after giving an instruction. However, this 'wait time' does accomplish two very important things. Firstly, it allows the children a few seconds grace to organise themselves. Secondly, it allows the teacher time to focus on what they want to see.

### Step 3. Look for appropriate behaviour.

**Look for children who have followed the instruction.**

Look for children who have followed the instruction.

Effective teachers understand that what they look for they very often find. Highly skilled operators of the 'Greens and Sandtraps' strategy have an ability to focus on and find appropriate behaviour. They're able to find just the one or two children out of a group who are first to follow an instruction — they may be the only ones!

...'Children are generally compliant little creatures once they know specifically what it is that you want'....

...Ancient Classroom Wisdom.

**Step 4. Acknowledge appropriate behaviour.**

Highly proficient teachers specifically acknowledge children who have chosen to follow their instruction. These teachers don't acknowledge appropriate behaviour using generic terms like 'Good boy/girl' or 'Well done'. They use behaviour-specific language. If the instruction was to line up quietly they will specifically acknowledge 'quiet lining up'.

In the classroom, the 'Greens and the Sandtraps' strategy might sound like this:

The teacher, ready to stop the lesson, says:

*Girls and boys, I'd like you to put your pens down and listen to me please.*

(This is **Step 1.**)

The teacher communicates her positive expectation of compliance in many subtle ways because her actions are congruent with her positive belief system — she acts as if the children will choose to follow her instruction.

Pause: (4 - 5 seconds) The teacher gives 'wait time' to allow the children time to begin following the instruction and to allow herself the opportunity to focus on and find appropriate behaviour. (These are **Steps 2 and 3.**)

Instead of choosing to focus on the Sandtraps (those who choose not to comply), she focuses on the Greens (children who choose to comply) and says:

> *Mary, thanks for putting your pen down quickly.*
>
> *John, it's great to see you listening quietly.*
>
> *Sue, I can see you're ready to listen to me, thank you.*
>
> *Mark, thanks for putting your pen down straight away.*

The teacher makes specific reference to her initial instruction (pens down, listen to me) while acknowledging appropriate behaviour. (This is **Step 4.**)

**...she acts as if the children will choose to follow her instruction.**

## The Hidden Bonus

The 'Greens and Sandtraps' strategy also has a hidden bonus besides its superb ability to provide teachers with a positive focus in their classrooms. Its other major asset lies in the fact that it also provides a positive cuing system for those children in the classroom who didn't respond to the teacher's instruction straight away. *Mary, thanks for putting your pen down quickly,* becomes a positively framed cue for Bob who was daydreaming when the instruction was given.

**...becomes a positively framed cue for Bob who was daydreaming**

The best practitioners of this 'Greens and Sandtraps' strategy use the hidden cuing strength of this technique to their great advantage. They might, for example, make specific reference to Sue, who is listening quietly, knowing she sits NEXT to Bob, who is 'off task' and daydreaming. Increasing the proximity of the positive cue to Bob increases the likelihood of Bob responding.

To have an even greater impact, the teacher may also choose to increase his/her physical proximity to the child who needs a positive cue for behaviour. The teacher notices that Bob has not followed his/her instruction so he/she says:

*John,* (John sits next to Bob) *thanks for putting your blue pen down straight away.*

The teacher moves casually in Bob's direction.

*Sue, I can see you're ready to listen, thank you.*

(Sue also sits next to Bob.)

The teacher is now standing non-threateningly near Bob's desk.

*Mark, terrific, your pen's down, you're ready to listen.*

The teacher notices that Bob has responded to the positive cue and takes the opportunity to acknowledge Bob's effort.

*Bob, great to see you're ready to listen, thank you.*

## Paraphrasing

If you paraphrase your initial instruction while acknowledging appropriate behaviour, you provide a positive cue for those children who didn't respond the first time **without actually having to repeat the instruction.** This is a more effective and more positive management strategy than:

> *Put your pens down and listen to me.*
>
> *Mary, put your pen down.*
>
> *I'm waiting for you John.*
>
> *Sue, I'm not continuing until everyone's listening.*
>
> *Hurry up, Mark.*

The 'Greens and Sandtraps' strategy is an amazingly powerful technique when used consistently in the classroom. On its own it can transform your teaching experience. I would encourage you to take my ten-day challenge, to test for yourself the value of what I'm suggesting. Follow the steps outlined above for just ten consecutive days and judge for yourself the effects on your classroom. Of course, having a positive focus is not something you have to restrict to your job. With a bit of persistence you may well change your whole life experience by focusing on the Greens!

### SUMMARY

- Just because you see things a certain way doesn't mean it is the right or only way to see things.
- What it is you look for you very often find.
- Effective teachers look for appropriate behaviour.
- Problems can be 'reframed'.
- The Greens and the Sandtraps strategy can help you look for and focus on positive classroom behaviour.

# CHAPTER 3

# Empowering Assumptions About Behaviour

Some of the most profound understandings I have about behaviour management have resulted from conversations with practising classroom teachers. There's a tremendous bank of untapped wisdom out there. These teachers don't have a degree in psychology but they do have a PhD in 'Results'.

These understandings or assumptions provide some of the major supports upon which the belief system, *Difficult doesn't mean impossible,* rests. On its own, each empowering assumption may not be able to provide enough strength to support a positive belief system, but together they are able to do so.

> …'We are what we think. All that we are arises with our thoughts. With our thoughts we create our world.'…
>
> …The Buddha.

I base my work on these *Four Empowering Assumptions.*

### Assumption 1

Behaviour is learned and new behaviour can be learned.

### Assumption 2

Behaviour is effective. It is most likely to be getting needs met, otherwise it wouldn't exist.

### Assumption 3

It is not the topography of behaviour that is important but what the behaviour is trying to communicate to you.

### Assumption 4

Behaviour is contextual.

## Behaviour is learned and new behaviours can be learned.

Some teachers assume that a child's behaviour is largely determined by their family background or their genetic make-up. As a result of their assumption they can't see the point in trying to teach a child new appropriate classroom behaviours. After all, they say, recidivism runs in the family. I've seen children in classrooms experience ongoing failure because a teacher's deterministic point of view stops him/her attempting to teach a new set of behaviours.

Highly skilled managers of challenging children are in the **learning** business. They look upon classroom behaviour in much the same way they look upon reading, 'riting and 'rithmetic - they're always looking for ways to help children learn what is not known. They work from the premise that just because a child doesn't know how to behave now doesn't mean he or she can't learn how to behave appropriately.

If you choose to adopt the point of view that **behaviour is learned and new behaviours can be learned**, then as a teacher you're in a very influential position because you're playing to your strength — helping children learn.

### The Bushtrack Theory

I like to think of behaviour and learning in terms of bushtracks.

The first time I venture into virgin bushland there are no paths or tracks for me to follow. To walk I have to push aside larger shrubs and perhaps even trample down a few grasses. My journey might leave a barely recognisable path in the countryside. The next time I choose to journey in this direction though, there will

**...you're playing to your strength—helping children learn.**

***Author's Note****: 'Bushtrack' is an Australian term used to describe unsealed roads and pathways which meander through the Australian outback and are created out of a need to make a pathway for traffic. A well-used bushtrack eventually becomes a road.*

**Each time a behaviour occurs it increases the likelihood that it will occur again...**

probably be a path of 'less resistance' available for me to follow. Each time I use the path, the wider and more recognisable it becomes as a path and the less resistance it offers me. As a consequence, this bushtrack becomes an easier and more inviting option for me as a walker. The learning of new behaviours takes place in much the same way. Each time a behaviour occurs it increases the likelihood that it will occur again as the neural connections are strengthened and a recognisable path of less resistance is formed out of the billions of possible neural pathways that are available. Unfortunately, some children come to our classes with veritable six-lane super highways of very well-established, inappropriate behaviours. These behaviours are well-worn as patterns and also offer the 'path of least resistance' to the child.

Using the 'Bushtrack' theory let's examine the case of Debbie, a young girl with behaviours severely inappropriate to the classroom setting. Debbie came from what psychologists would call a 'dysfunctional' home. In class she would bite, kick and hit. Debbie had come to school with some completely inappropriate bushtracks. You can imagine the stress this was causing the teachers and the other children.

Eventually, a case conference was called and a number of professionals were brought together to discuss how we could stop this 'problematic' behaviour. This group was trying to close down the inappropriate bushtracks Debbie had established.

Part-way through the meeting a young social worker (with the courage of her convictions) astutely pointed out to us that if we *were* somehow to close down Debbie's bushtracks and stop her having the option of choosing to behave in these ways (biting, kicking, hitting), we may well be placing her in a difficult, if not dangerous, position. Biting, kicking and hitting were Debbie's 'tools of survival' in the home setting. Take these options, these bushtracks, away from Debbie and who knows what the results would be. Debbie's problem wasn't the inappropriate behaviour, it was that she was using the bushtrack 'surviving at home' for 'surviving at school' which put her on the wrong path. Unfortunately, she had no other choice because she had never been provided the opportunity to develop any other tracks and therefore she saw no other options available to her. Debbie's biting, kicking and hitting behaviours were successful strategies for survival in the home setting but were completely out of context in the school. Behaviours that are inappropriate in one setting may achieve results in another.

Like Debbie, we all have bushtracks that are appropriate only to a particular context or setting. If I were to use the bushtracks appropriate to 'being with my friends' at a formal principals' meeting, I'd be out of a job or arrested.

We began to understand that what Debbie needed was help to develop new bushtracks. She needed new options and new choices that would enrich her life both in and out of school.

Suddenly, the whole focus of the case conference changed. Instead of looking for ways to stop Debbie behaving badly, we searched for ways to help Debbie generate new behaviours she could use in the classroom. Suddenly, we were in the business of *generative change*. Thanks to the dedication and commitment of the school staff, Debbie learned many new behaviours appropriate to the class setting.

Inappropriate behaviour is a *context* problem. Working from the assumption that *behaviour is learned,* effective teachers help children generate new bushtracks/behaviours that are appropriate in the context of the classroom.

**Behaviours that are inappropriate in one setting may achieve results in another.**

**Flexibility of behaviour is one of the keys to success in life.**

Flexibility of behaviour is one of the keys to success in life. In other words, if you're doing something and find it's not working, but you have the flexibility of behaviour to try new and varied strategies, then the more strategies you can try the more likely you are to experience success. Alternatively, if you're doing something and it's not working, but you don't have the flexibility of behaviour to try something else - then you are doomed to failure.

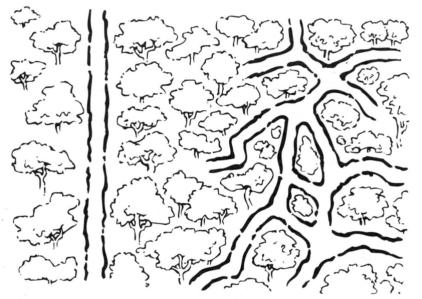

Children, like adults, need choices and options. The more choices and options they have, the more flexible their behaviour will be and the more flexible their behaviour is, the more likely they are to experience success both in and out of school.

### The Key to Generative Change

There's no doubt that new classroom bushtracks are often hard to generate. However, highly resourceful teachers have found a way to maximise the chances that they are able to help children with this difficult task. These teachers are aware of the *effect on* and the *power of* their attention on classroom behaviour. Effective teachers pay maximum attention to appropriate behaviour and minimum attention to inappropriate behaviour.

**...pay maximum attention to appropriate behaviour and minimum attention to inappropriate behaviour.**

A well-known piece of research, conducted many years ago, suitably illustrates the effect and power teachers have when managing classroom behaviour. The experiment was carried out with rats that were placed in different situations and had their behaviour closely observed.

In the first case, rats were placed in a cage with a lever at one end. When the lever was pushed a movie was screened onto the wall at one end of the cage. The rats found this reinforcing and continued to press the lever.

This led psychologists to **learning principle number one**.

> *Intelligent creatures, like rats and children, like to have something to do — it helps their brains grow.*

In the second case, the rats were placed in a cage with nothing to do. This situation led to behaviour brought about by the lack of alternative activities and included the rubbing off of fur and a high level of sexual behaviour.

This led psychologists to **learning principle number two**.

> *Intelligent creatures, like rats and children, will do anything to keep from being bored — including some things we would call silly or destructive.*

In the third case, the rats received a mild, harmless electric shock every few minutes which was sufficient to make them feel uncomfortable.

To conclude the experiment the rats were given choice as to which cage they preferred. Naturally, cage one was the first choice of the rats. Interestingly, the second choice of the rats was the cage containing the electric shock which led psychologists to the **most important learning principle** of all,

> *Intelligent creatures, like rats and children, would rather have bad things happen to them than nothing at all.*

It seems that some teachers believe that there are two types of attention: positive attention that increases good behaviour and negative attention that decreases good behaviour.

Unfortunately, this is not the case at all!

In our classrooms many of us are 'unwitting behaviour modifiers' because we give children too much attention for inappropriate behaviour and not enough attention for appropriate behaviour. The least effective way of managing behaviour is to tell a child what it is he or she is doing wrong — even if you do it in a loving and caring way. Constantly telling Tess to sit down when she is out of her seat is not likely to increase 'in-seat behaviour'. If you want to increase the time Tess spends in her chair, you need to catch her when she's SITTING and acknowledge this appropriate behaviour.

**If you want to increase the time Tess spends in her chair, you need to catch her when she's SITTING and acknowledge this appropriate behaviour.**

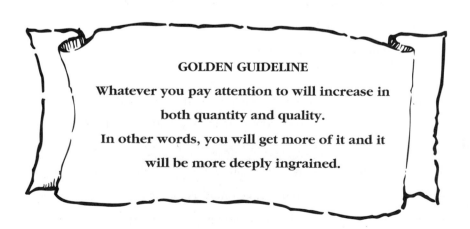

**GOLDEN GUIDELINE**
**Whatever you pay attention to will increase in both quantity and quality.**
**In other words, you will get more of it and it will be more deeply ingrained.**

Helping children create new classroom bushtracks is a lengthy process, a step-by-step job. It isn't best done by constantly telling children they're behaving inappropriately or by punishing them for being on an incorrect bushtrack. It's most proficiently done by *leading and supporting appropriate classroom behaviour.* This way children get the feedback and encouragement they need to create a whole new way of doing things.

New bushtracks don't just appear out of nowhere, fully formed and ready for children to use. They take time and effort to establish, develop and maintain. It's highly unlikely a child will abandon a well-worn, well-established track and spontaneously develop a new path just because you suddenly start paying maximum attention to appropriate behaviour and minimum attention to inappropriate behaviour. Bushwalking is a difficult pursuit and we all get especially tired pushing aside grasses and shrubs on our first venture into uncharted territory. It's more likely that we'll only get part-way to our destination on our first attempt. We have made an effort, towards our original goal, and been partly successful. If we feel we are on the correct path we will return to try again and this time the first leg of our journey will be slightly less strenuous. With continued encouragement and practice we will eventually achieve our goal and establish a whole new track which we can choose to use any time we feel it is correct to do so. Success can often appear to be an 'overnight' phenomenon, but it is more usually the result of improved approximations over time. Children learn new behaviours in much the same way. Effective teachers notice and support approximations of appropriate classroom behaviour. They act **as if** the child already has a well-worn and well-established appropriate bushtrack. In this way they encourage children to return to this barely recognisable track and allow them to work on establishing a well-worn bushtrack over time.

**Effective teachers notice and support approximations of appropriate classroom behaviour.**

For example, Mark's teacher notices Mark (who constantly calls out) half raising his hand and immediately takes the opportunity to encourage and support the beginnings of a tentative new bushtrack. He/she says, *Mark it's great to see your hand up, thanks for waiting. What do you think?*

Teachers who wish to make an impact work from the premise that behaviour is learned and new behaviours can be learned. They aim to create new bushtracks/options for children by noticing and supporting appropriate classroom behaviour.

## ASSUMPTION 2

## Behaviour is effective. It's most likely to be getting needs met, otherwise it wouldn't exist.

I try not to use the terms 'good' and 'bad' to describe behaviour any more. 'Effective' is my preferred term for describing behaviour these days. However 'good' or 'bad' classroom behaviour may appear to us (remember, we don't GET meanings we CREATE them), we can be confident that the behaviour is effective in helping someone to get his or her needs met. This is the prime reason the behaviour continues to exist. A baby who cries at 3 a.m. because he/she is hungry or wet is not behaving in a 'bad' or 'naughty' way, but simply using the most effective behaviour at his/her disposal. The result is that Mum or Dad has to get out of bed, but also that the baby's needs are met.

My friend Scott has a little boy called Paul. I was visiting Scott just recently and we were having one of our 'state of the world' discussions under the shade of a spreading fig tree. Halfway through the conversation it became abundantly clear that Paul wanted his bike fixed.

PAUL:    *Daaad, will you fix my bike please? It's busted. Will you Dad?*
SCOTT:   *Not now, mate, I'm talking to Gerry.*
PAUL:    *But Dad, I'm bored, I want to play. Please, Dad.*

SCOTT:   *Listen, Paul, this is important, I'll look later.*

PAUL :   *My bike's important too, Dad - please.'*

SCOTT:   *NO!*

PAUL :   *SSCCRREEAAMM*

SCOTT:   *HEY, that's no way to behave. Here, be quiet and let me have a quick look.*

As a bystander interested in human behaviour I was impressed with Paul's ability to get his needs met through the use of very effective behaviour. Paul had a goal in mind — get his bike fixed — and he tried a variety of strategies to motivate Scott into action: asking nicely, persisting and finally yelling as loudly as he could. Interestingly, it was the strategy described by Scott as, 'no way to behave' that seemed to do the trick.

Scott would no doubt describe Paul's behaviour as 'bad' or 'naughty' and would scoff at my suggestion that it would best be described as highly effective. Likewise, I'll probably get the same reaction when I suggest to Tess's teacher that her 'out-of-seat behaviour' is highly effective in getting her needs met, too.

Behaviour is effective, that's why it's so difficult to generate new bushtracks. What motivation is there for Paul to stop screaming when it's *so effective at getting the job done and his needs met?*

**Behaviour is effective, that's why it's so difficult to generate new bushtracks.**

Have you ever noticed how supermarket chains target parents with young children by placing chocolate bars right near the check-out? Market research tells them that children's behaviour at check-outs is highly effective in getting their needs for chocolate met. I often wonder what would happen to such forms of highly effective behaviour if parents were to gaze admiringly at their screaming offspring and say, 'That is almost highly effective behaviour, my sweet'.

In the classroom, if you can remember to look at children's behaviour in terms of its effectiveness rather than in terms of its 'goodness' or 'badness', you're going to create a whole new perspective for yourself. You'll begin to see possibilities for teaching new context-appropriate ways to help children get their needs met.

Of course the spin-off is that you're very likely to get your needs met too.

**ASSUMPTION 3**

### It is not the topography of behaviour that is important but what the behaviour is trying to communicate to you.

A short time ago I was working as a supply teacher in a difficult English inner city school. Halfway through a thrilling lesson on improper fractions chaos broke out in the class next door.  My lesson stopped and as I stuck my head out of the classroom door to investigate, I spotted Rory in the corridor.

> *Rory*, I said, *What's going on?*
> *I bit Freddy,* he replied nonchalantly.
> *Why did you bite Freddy?* I naively asked.
> *Mum comes to take me home when I bite someone,* came the straightforward answer.

I remember having one of those 'aha' moments when I realised that it wasn't the 'biting Freddy' that's important but the 'I want to go home'. Most of us, as teachers, would understandably get caught up with the topography of the behaviour (what the behaviour looks like — the biting) and not *listen* to what the behaviour is trying to communicate to us - *I want to go home.*

**...effective teachers choose to listen to what children's behaviour is trying to tell them.**

I've learned that effective teachers choose to listen to what children's behaviour is trying to tell them.

Often the clearest messages behind children's behaviours are things like:

- 'I'm anxious.'
- 'I'm bored.'
- 'I'm worried/stressed/angry/jealous.'
- 'Notice me.'
- 'Fight with me.'

A great strategy that some teachers use to help them 'listen' to the messages behind behaviour, I call the BBQ technique.

## THE BBQ TECHNIQUE

A BBQ is a **B**rilliantly **B**etter **Q**uestion that focuses on solutions instead of problems.

*What's this behaviour trying to tell me?* instead of *What did I do to deserve this?*

*How can I listen more carefully to the message behind this child's behaviour?* instead of

*What's wrong with this child?*

Because questions are the answers, asking yourself a **Brilliantly Better Question** will always lead you to a **Brilliantly Better Answer**.

I recall watching a marvellous teacher working with a young girl who required a lot of educational support in the classroom. Things seemed to go well for about 20 minutes, then all hell would break loose. Books would fly off the table, pens and pencils would get broken and a banshee-like cry would fill the room. This was a fairly consistent pattern of behaviour.

Quite naturally, I got fairly caught up in the heat of the moment and became focused on the topography of the behaviour (the throwing of a

**The teacher focused on what the behaviour might be trying to *communicate* to her.**

tantrum). The teacher, on the other hand, focused on what the behaviour might be trying to *communicate* to her. She asked herself a BBQ. She asked herself, *This is happening too often, what is this girl trying to say to me?*

She deduced that the message behind the behaviour was 'I need a break!' So, she organized a mini-recess for her student every 18 minutes: a toilet break, a drink and a two-minute walk.

The throwing of tantrums completely stopped. The teacher had successfully inferred the message behind the behaviour. She then rearranged the environment, thus allowing the child to have her needs met.

Perhaps the next time you find yourself caught up in the topography of the behaviour, feeling angry or perhaps frustrated, you can try to change your focus and listen to the message behind the behaviour by using the BBQ technique.

**...to be sensitive enough to 'listen' to what the child is trying to communicate...**

Often the easiest and most successful way of dealing with challenging behaviour is to be sensitive enough to 'listen' to what the child is trying to communicate to you and then to rearrange the environment so as to try to meet this need. I call this the *today* part of the intervention. The *tomorrow* part of the intervention is to help the child to open up new bushtracks that will allow him or her to successfully deal with the environment that originally caused so much difficulty.

## ASSUMPTION 4

### Behaviour is Contextual.

A major problem we face in trying to come to terms with challenging behaviour is that our traditions of analysis were set out long before we knew anything about 'systems behaviour'. Nevertheless, there have always been teachers who sensed that when something is analysed into its parts, much of the original is lost. There are qualities and attributes that only exist when all the parts are put together in a system. When we analyse something into its parts we learn something, but we must always be aware of how much we are missing. Behaviour is contextual. It arises in response to specific people and specific places. One of the biggest mistakes you can make as a behaviour manager is to try to understand a child's classroom behaviour in isolation, because it can't be done. Behaviour exists as part of a system and the classroom is one of the most complex systems I know.

**Behaviour is contextual. It arises in response to specific people and specific places.**

Physicists know virtually everything there is to know about the water molecule. One large oxygen atom with two smaller hydrogen atoms attached to it. It is the 'Mickey Mouse' of the molecular world. Its behaviour is governed by well-understood equations of atomic physics. But when you put a few zillion of these molecules together in the same pot, suddenly you've got something that shimmers and gurgles and sloshes. These zillions of molecules have collectively acquired a property, liquidity, that none of them possesses alone. There's nothing in those well-understood equations of atomic physics that even hints at such a property. 'Liquidity' is an emergent property.

Just because a physicist can describe a water molecule in minute detail doesn't mean for one second that he/she would presume to be describing water. Likewise, just because you think you know everything there is to know about a child doesn't mean you can predict his or her behaviour in the classroom. Behaviours will emerge in response to all other parts of the classroom system. You can think that you know everything there is to know about ten individuals and yet be completely surprised by the behaviours that EMERGE when they form a group. The ability to know everything there is to know about 30 individuals does not imply the

**.........be completely surprised by the behaviours that EMERGE when they form a group.**

ability to start from this knowledge and reconstruct a classroom or the behaviour of the children in that class. From the interaction of the individual components down here (molecules, neurons, consumers, children) emerges some kind of **global property** up there (liquidity, the brain, the 'economy', classroom behaviour), something you couldn't have predicted from what you know of the component parts. This emergent **global property** feeds back to influence the individuals down here who produced it.

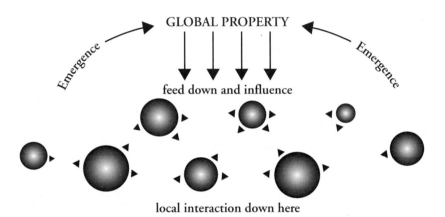

**Classroom behaviour is the EMERGENT property of a group of individuals interacting together.**

Classroom behaviour is the EMERGENT property of a group of individuals interacting together. To view a child's behaviour in isolation from the system in which it emerges is to ignore all that can only be seen when the parts are together.

A child's behaviour emerges in response to specific people and specific places and any classroom care and discipline program must take into account those people and those places.

To attempt to view and then to manage a child's behaviour in isolation from the system in which it takes place is to fall for the *'reductionist' trap.*

...'Make no mistake, to understand the earth, how GAIA works, requires a top down view, a view of the earth as a whole system, if you like, as something alive. It is no use gathering together meteorologists, biologists, marine scientists, atmospheric chemists and so on in one place and expecting results. Because of their training they will always be 'reductionists' and take a bottom-up view — a view that assumes the whole is never more than the sum of its parts and that by taking things apart we can find out how they work.

We need science, but it must grow from the top down.'...

... James Lovelock.

For about 300 years we have lived in a clockwork and predictable universe described for us by Sir Isaac Newton. Classical thought was that when sufficiently powerful analytical tools were eventually at hand, we would unlock the hidden secrets of life. The central discovery of recent years is that this is just not so. The universe is in a state of constant change, containing many components interacting in complex ways which leads to notorious 'unpredictability'. Cause and effect are not the useful tools they once used to be.

**Cause and effect are not the useful tools they once used to be.**

For example, I wake up one morning with a splitting headache. A traffic jam causes me to be late for work where an unusually busy and difficult day awaits me. My boss is offhand with me and uncharacteristically short-tempered. I get a flat tyre on the way home and have to fix it in the pouring rain. The supermarket is sold out of the ingredients I need to make dinner. Arriving home near exhaustion, the dog runs out to greet me and as he jumps up he is severely scolded and bellowed at.

41

Using a linear, causative approach and not taking into account the day's complex web of interactions, we might say that the dog was scolded because it jumped up: 'A' causes 'B'.

A non-linear approach allows for the day's web of events that finally led to the emergent behaviour of the dog being scolded.

Traditionally, to find a solution we have tried to define the problem. However, the world is too complex and ever-changing. If we continue to look for cause and effect we will fail to understand much of the nature of the situation. Believing that problem behaviour can be linked to one or two factors is failing to see the interconnection of all the factors that work to influence our daily lives.

**If we continue to look for cause and effect we will fail to understand much of the nature of the situation.**

cause and effect

You only have to think of the number of times that **you** have heard, *The problem is that his mum and dad let him run wild* or, *He's fine at home, it's just that those teachers don't know how to handle him.*

In these sorts of situations finding solutions becomes less important than deferring responsibility or assigning blame. Accomplished classroom teachers manage the classroom the way they do because they are **system thinkers** and they view the classroom as a complex, non-linear, interrelated web of interactions. They are wary of simple cause and effect explanations for behaviour.

There are many factors influencing behaviour in the complex, interrelated world in which we live. They do not operate alone but in interrelationship with us and with each other. If one factor changes, then all parts will readjust and change too. A traffic accident is a great example of a complex interrelated 'event'. On a wet and slippery road an accident occurs. The southbound traffic is halted for about 15 minutes as police work to remove the vehicles. Because it's a busy road, traffic begins to bank up during this 15-minute period. In fact, it banks up for a number of kilometres. Moving this backlog of traffic is slower than the rate at which new traffic joins the end of the queue. The queue gets longer. It is no longer the original accident causing the queue but the queue itself. Traffic lights along the southbound route mean that traffic does not move off too quickly and the lights on other parts of the system react to heavier than usual traffic on one road by slowing down traffic on others. The backlog continues. Curious drivers on the northbound lanes slow to have a quick look at the situation. It's only over the course of many hours that the system works to smooth out the jam that only took a few minutes to actually clear. In many ways, the world of human beings is like the world of traffic lights. A change in one part of the system feeds into all its other parts. A small ripple eventually spreads over the whole pond. A change in one part of the classroom can often cause dramatic and unpredictable changes on all other parts of the system. In many cases this change can ripple even further and affect changes in the whole school environment and eventually even into the home and the community.

Effective teachers are **systems thinkers**. They are aware that the classroom system behaves in ways common to all other complex systems. All systems are in a constant state of change. Sometimes these changes are large and sometimes these changes are small. Physicists interested in the behaviour of complex systems have a vivid metaphor to demonstrate this phenomenon. Imagine a pile of sand on a tabletop, with a steady drizzle of new grains raining down from above. The pile grows higher and higher until it can't grow any more: old sand is cascading down the sides and off the edge of the table as fast as new sand drizzles down. The resulting sand pile is *self-organised,* in that it reaches a specific shape without any outside *control* and without anyone explicitly shaping it. The sand pile is also in a state of *'criticality',* in the sense that the sand

**All systems are in a constant state of change.**

grains are barely stable. The microscopic surfaces and edges of the grains are interlocked in every conceivable combination, and are just ready to give way. So when a falling grain hits there is **no telling what will happen**; maybe nothing, maybe just a tiny shift in a few grains. Or maybe, if one tiny collision leads to another in just the right chain reaction, a catastrophic landslide will take off one whole face of the sand pile. In fact, ALL these things do happen at one time or another. Big avalanches are rare, small ones are more frequent.

This systems behaviour is common in nature. It can be seen in the activity of the sun or the stock market, through the fossil records, in the flow of current through a resistor, in the flow of water through a river and in the interactions that take place in the classroom system. Effective teachers are prepared emotionally for the small trickles and the BIG avalanches because they will occur — it's just a naturally expressed law of systems behaviour.

A little girl was at her dressing table while her father was working on the word processor in the room next door. He could hear frustrated grunts and groans of disapproval coming from his daughter's room for what seemed like hours. Finally, his curiosity got the better of him and he abandoned his task to find out what the cause of the frustration was. He found his daughter admiring a newly tidied dressing table. With only a dozen items on the dresser he began to wonder why the task had taken her so long. He asked his daughter and she didn't know, she just remarked that it was a difficult job. The father took one item, moved it and said, *What happens if I put the brush here? It's wrong,* his daughter replied. *Well, what happens if I put your bracelet here? That's wrong too,* she said. Each time the father tried to move one of the items he was quickly assured that 'it's wrong'.  It was then that the father realised why his daughter had found the task so frustrating and why it had taken her so long. She had only one way for the desk to be right and **endless possibilities** for it to be wrong. The world of the classroom is complex and ever-changing. If you only have *one way for your room to be right*, you are setting up yourself and the children in your room for continued frustration and failure. Life in the classroom is a random event and adaptability and flexibility are the keys to survival.

Skilled teachers understand that the classroom is a complex, unpredictable, 'messy', non-linear working environment. They have never tried to pretend that they are ever in control of it because they realised long ago that **control is an illusion.**

**...control is an illusion.**

## SUMMARY

***Assumption 1:*** Behaviour is learned and new behaviour can be learned.

- Assumptions can empower or 'disempower' us when we are faced with challenging behaviour.
- One empowering assumption is that behaviour is learned and new behaviours can be learned.
- The bushtrack theory is a powerful metaphor for thinking about how behaviour is learned.
- Generative change is about opening new bushtracks rather than closing down old ones.

***Assumption 2:*** Behaviour is effective. It is most likely to be getting needs met, otherwise it wouldn't exist.

- Children behave the way they do in our classrooms because it has proved effective in getting their needs met.
- We find some children challenging and label them 'bad', but the moment we do so, we close down our options for helping children get their needs met appropriately.

***Assumption 3:*** It is not the topography of behaviour that is important but what the behaviour is trying to communicate to you.

- The unspoken message behind challenging behaviour is more important than what the behaviour looks like.
- BBQs focus on solutions rather than problems.
- Asking yourself a BBQ will lead you to a BBA.
- Often the most successful way of dealing with challenging behaviour is to be sensitive enough to listen to what the behaviour is trying to communicate. Rearrange the environment in an attempt to meet the needs of the challenging behaviour. Tomorrow you will have to help the child generate new bushtracks to deal with the environment that caused so much trouble.

***Assumption 4:*** Behaviour is contextual.

- A child's behaviour can not be viewed in isolation from the setting in which it takes place. It emerges in response to the setting.
- Disciplines such as physics, economics, biology and sociology have long been aware of the nature of systems behaviour. They have a lot to teach us about the classroom as a complex system and how we can best work with it.

# CHAPTER 4

# The Illusion of Control

Relaxing over a lazy Sunday brunch I came across an article in a local paper written by a leading educator. It was titled, *Teachers Must Regain Control of Their Classrooms*. The title of the article alone was enough to make me flinch. Sure enough, by the time I had finished reading I felt a genuine sense of concern for any teacher following the advice that it contained.

Imagine encouraging teachers to 'regain' control of something that they never really had control of in the first place!

While at teacher training college, I was taught about the ABCs of behaviour. The ABC model is one that psychologists frequently use when talking about classroom behaviour. Basically, the model looked like this:

**A**: is the **A**ntecedents to behaviour, or
what sets the stage;

**B**: is the **B**ehaviour itself; and

**C**: is the **C**onsequences of behaviour.

With this model of behaviour in mind I want to identify two broad models of teaching I have observed in classrooms.

**Model 1** teachers are those who try to control the only thing they have no real control over — *other people's behaviour*. With the best of intentions they invest extraordinarily large amounts of time and energy into trying to control the only part of the ABC equation they can't control, the Bs — other people's behaviour.

Despite all their efforts at *control* they achieve very little besides giving themselves the beginnings of an ulcer and experiencing a growing sense of frustration.

**Model 2** teachers invest time and energy into controlling the As and the Cs of the equation. Most importantly they concentrate on the Cs — and in particular their own behaviour. They focus on their own behaviour because they realise that it's the only part of the equation over which they have **total control.**

**...they concentrate on the C's — and in particular their own behaviour.**

## An Efficient Model of Control

Imagine if you will one huge traffic jam of problems in the classroom represented by all these cars.

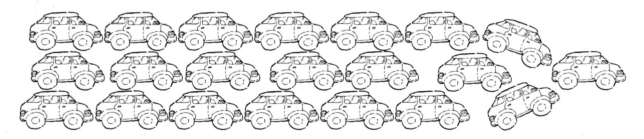

To clear the traffic jam there are a select few key cars in which we will be interested; the rest we will have no special interest in at all. We can represent the select few we are interested in by colouring a small number of cars black.

Among the select few cars we are interested in, there are even fewer cars over which we have any real control. We can represent the car over which we have any real control by shading one car black.

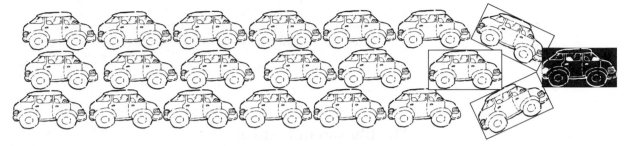

To help clear the 'traffic jams' that occur regularly in the classroom, highly effective teachers focus on the only car over which they have any control — the one they are driving. Effective teachers focus on things they can do something about — and it is always their own behaviour.

**Effective teachers focus on things they can do something about – and it is always their own behaviour.**

Reactive teachers concentrate their efforts on cars which may be of interest but over which they have no control. They focus on the behaviour of other people, the problems in the wider school environment and other circumstances over which they have no real control. Looking at other people's problems can result in a feeling of helplessness in the teacher, a feeling of victimisation and the development of a 'siege mentality' characterised by feelings of 'us against them'.

The way highly resourceful teachers talk about CONTROL is a clear indicator of just what their focus is. These teachers have a model of control that grows from the inside-out. They focus on themselves and their own behaviour first. Their language is couched in phrases such as:

*How can I be more positive?*
*How can I be more resourceful?*
*How can I build better rapport with Geoff?*

They focus on their 'area of control' and from their area of control they then seek to positively influence all other parts of the complex system that makes up the classroom.

The learned gentleman who wrote the article that had so concerned me had fallen for one of the most powerful illusions of the teaching profession.

## The Illusion of Control

Control is an illusion. You can not control another person's behaviour. Although the illusion of control is extremely powerful, look at the two **false assumptions** upon which it stands.

*Assumption 1:* The assumption that anyone could master and control a dynamic complex system like the classroom from the top.

*Assumption 2:* The assumption that giving orders and being in control are one and the same thing - *because they are not!*

Highly accomplished teachers don't use a **model of control** in their classrooms, instead they teach using a **model of influence**. The **model of influence** is much more effective than the model of control **because it works**! It's based on a systems approach to classroom management where the teacher focuses on his or her area of control to lead and support positive behaviour.

## The Model of Control (The 'Outside-In' model)

- Teacher seen as 'Outside' or 'Above' the classroom system.
- Teacher tries to 'Control' from outside or above and is met with resistance.
- Net effect is ZERO. It's like two evenly matched tug-o-war teams pitched against each other.

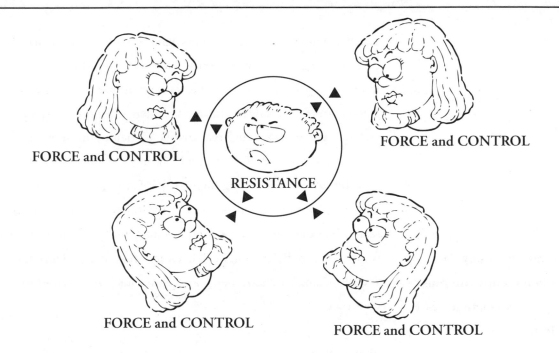

FORCE and CONTROL

RESISTANCE

FORCE and CONTROL

FORCE and CONTROL

FORCE and CONTROL

## The Model of Influence (The 'Inside-Out' model)

- Teacher seen as an 'Influential' part of the system.
- Teacher understands that change in any one part of the system can lead to changes in all other parts of the system.
- Teacher focuses on controlling the only part of the system that he/she can control: *his/her own behaviour.*

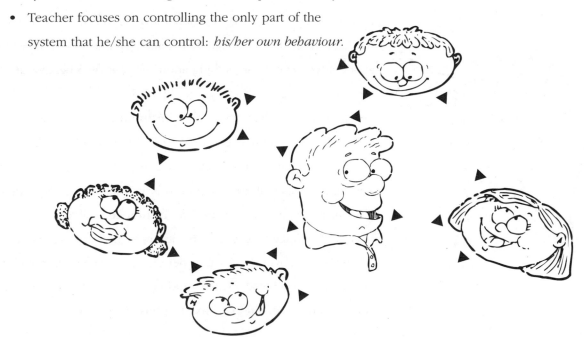

Teachers who are 'systems thinkers' have a highly effective approach to causing change in their classrooms. They understand that causing change in any one part of an interconnected system like the classroom leads automatically to changes and readjustments in all other parts of the system. Therefore, to cause real change in their rooms they focus firstly on changing the one thing over which they have any control — **their own behaviour.** Watching highly capable teachers use this 'model of influence' based on the 'Inside-Out' approach to change I have come to realise that there is now a starting point I always begin from when I want to change behaviour. I call it 'Gerry's first rule' and it states: If you want to change a child's behaviour, you must be prepared to change your own first.

**If you want to change a child's behaviour, you must be prepared to change your own first.**

Abandoning the 'illusion of control' is one of the most difficult things for a classroom teacher to do. Many of us feel the need for a sense of 'power over', or 'control of', our classrooms. Yet once you realise you can only control and be held accountable for your own behaviour you will feel a tremendous sense of relief and wellbeing.

**...you will feel a tremendous sense of relief and wellbeing.**

At last you don't have to bluff, bully or bribe to keep the illusion alive. All that mental and emotional involvement can now be directed into an area that you can do something about — your own behaviour.

Teachers often underestimate their **influence** on the children in their care. A teacher's influence extends into the home. They affect periods of time that children normally spend with their families and friends. Through activities like homework, discussions of the day's events in obvious and more subtle ways, the **influence** of teachers on the lives of children is incredible. Teachers must recognise that their beliefs about themselves, the world and other people affect the children with whom they come into contact. This would be a step towards a more honest and humane recognition of the responsibilities involved in teaching.

The size of class, the size of the budget, access to resources, the number and quality of textbooks are all far less *influential* than the teacher.

In the following chapters we will examine how it is that wonderfully effective teachers focus on their own behaviour to influence challenging children in their classrooms.

## The Classroom Continuum

A classroom, like any other complex system (a living creature, an ecosystem, an economy, the universe), is in a constant state of flux and change. Like any other system, it engages in periods of order and disorder.

Take water, cool it and you'll get ice, heat it and you'll get steam. As ice, the $H_2O$ molecules have almost no momentum and are in a state of inertia. As steam, the molecules rush around madly, colliding with one another. Too much heat results in *chaos*, too little heat results in *inertia*. *Water exists on a continuum between chaos and inertia.*

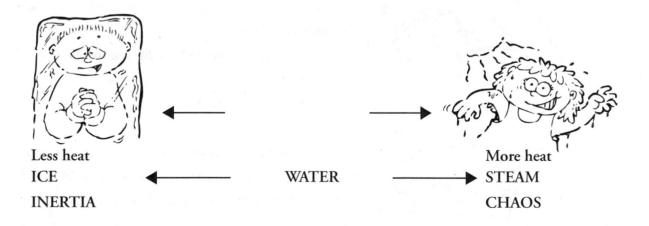

**Less heat**                         **More heat**
ICE         ⟵   WATER   ⟶   STEAM
INERTIA                               CHAOS

A manageable classroom also exists somewhere on the emotional continuum between inertia and chaos. Too much 'emotional heat' results in **chaos**. Not enough 'emotional heat' results in **inertia**.

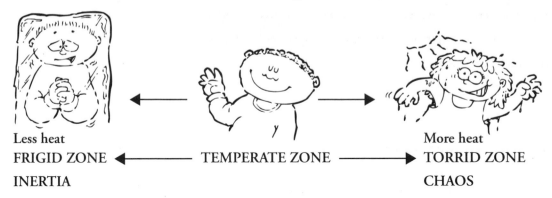

**Less heat**
**FRIGID ZONE** ⬅————— **TEMPERATE ZONE** —————➡ **TORRID ZONE**
**INERTIA**                                                    **CHAOS**

Problems occur most rapidly in classrooms where a teacher sees himself/ herself as separate to the process that moves a classroom from one 'zone' to another. Many teachers have mastered the art of keeping the classroom in the temperate zone. We have already looked at some of the ways these teachers 'keep it temperate'. They include:

- using non-linear, 'systems' view of management;
- using a model of teaching based on influence and not control;
- using an 'inside-out' approach to change which focuses on their own behaviour first;
- focusing on the **greens** and not the **sandtraps**;
- acting **as if**; and
- asking themselves a **BBQ**.

I call one other important strategy that highly able teachers use to 'keep it temperate' in their classrooms the 'old 1, 2, 3' strategy. The 'old 1, 2, 3' strategy is a highly-specific BBQ that the great managers of challenging behaviour ask themselves before they take any action regarding the children's behaviour.

Before successful teachers act, they take the time to decide whether a child's behaviour is at level 1, 2 or 3.

**Level 1:** The child is on task and is following all instructions (watch out for flying pigs).

**Level 2:** The child is 'off task' but non-disruptive. In other words, they may not be doing exactly what you want them to do but they are not stopping other children from learning or you from teaching (unless YOU chose to stop teaching to deal with them, in which case you have turned a level 2 behaviour into a level 3 behaviour).

**Level 3:** The child is actively disruptive and is stopping other children from learning and/or you from teaching.

Knowing whether a behaviour is at level 1, 2 or 3 can make a big difference to the way you deal with it. Modelling this strategy, I now always ask myself, 'Is this behaviour stopping me from teaching or any child from learning?'. If the answer is **No**, I know that I can afford to pay minimum attention to the behaviour. I'm now aware that many of the strategies that I previously used to try to move a child from a level 3 to level 2 or from a level 2 to level 1 behaviour did not work. In hindsight, they couldn't have worked because they focused on what the child was doing wrong instead of what the child was doing right. Highly proficient teachers are not 'unwitting behaviour modifiers' and they are acutely aware that the least effective way of dealing with behaviour is to tell the child what he or she is doing wrong.

Fred, who was sitting by the blackboard, began to draw on it and distract others. The teacher had a choice — to stop teaching and bring Fred 'into line' or to move slowly to the back of the class, away from Fred so as to take the attention of the other children with him. The teacher chose the second option to keep a level 2 behaviour at a level 2 rather than have it possibly escalate to level 3.

**Before successful teachers act, they take the time to decide whether a child's behaviour is at level 1, 2 or 3.**

**'Is this behaviour stopping me from teaching or any child from learning?'**

There is no magic involved in successfully dealing with level 1, 2 or 3 behaviours or in keeping classrooms in the 'temperate zone'. Effective teachers use a clearly observable and describable strategy, which I call the 'Big Toe First' technique.

**SUMMARY**

- Control is an illusion. You can not control another person's behaviour.

- Effective teachers have an 'Inside-Out' approach to change that focuses on controlling their own behaviour.

- Through the control they have over their own behaviour, teachers can influence, in a positive way, all other parts of the classroom system.

- A manageable classroom exists on a continuum with inertia at one end and chaos at the other.

- Teachers are a vital part of the process that moves a classroom along the continuum in either direction.

- The 'old 1, 2, 3' strategy is a great way to help keep it temperate.

- If you want to change a child's behaviour you have to be prepared to change your own first.

# CHAPTER 5

# The 'Big Toe First' Technique

C apable behaviour managers never jump in at the deep end when there's a chance of wading in from the shallows. They only venture into deeper waters when they have to, because their frays in the shallows have failed to positively correct a situation. They always test the water with their 'big toe first'.

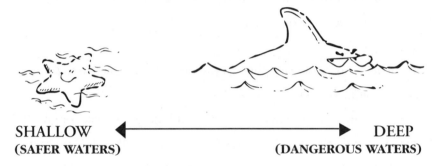

**SHALLOW**
**(SAFER WATERS)**　　　　　　　　**DEEP**
**(DANGEROUS WATERS)**

Effective Teachers Move Along this Continuum

Accomplished teachers take the following steps to ensure they start from the safer shallows and move slowly into more dangerous deep waters.

### Step 1 - Acknowledge appropriate behaviour.

Effective teachers acknowledge the appropriate behaviour of a child who is in close proximity to the targeted child. The appropriate behaviour acts as a model and acknowledging it acts as a positive cue for the child who has not followed the teacher's instruction (the greens and sandtraps). The closer the acknowledged behaviour to the targeted child, the greater the effect.

**...appropriate behaviour acts as a model and acknowledging it acts as a positive cue...**

The teacher notices that Mary is 'off task' and, using a positive cuing strategy, says, *Jack* (Jack sits next to Mary), *it's lovely to see you working quietly on the word processor.*

### Step 2 - Increase physical proximity.

Effective teachers increase their physical proximity to the targeted child (off-task child) while acknowledging appropriate classroom behaviour.

The teacher observes that Bill has not followed her instruction and using a positive cuing strategy says, *Clint* (Clint sits next to Bill), *thanks for putting your science book away quickly.*

The teacher moves casually towards Bill. *Mary* (sits near Bill), *it's great to see your science book away.*

The teacher increases her physical proximity to Bill and says, *Tom* (sits next to Bill), *you're ready, thank you.*
Note: She gives no negatives. She does not hold eye contact or give Bill 'the look'. Bill responds to the cues and the teacher takes the opportunity to acknowledge his cooperation by saying, *Bill, thanks for putting your books away.*

### Step 3 - A brief private question.

The teacher uses a brief private question to clarify any misunderstanding and to focus the child's attention on the task at hand. The teacher may approach a child quietly from the side, lower to his/her level and, without invading his/her personal space, say;

*Can I help you make a start, Todd?*
*Christine, is there something you don't understand?*
*Mark, how are you progressing?*

The teacher chooses to let Todd, Christine or Mark know she is pleased to see them working by acknowledging them—as soon as she 'catches' them working.

## Step 4 - A private direction.

The teacher gives a brief, simple and private direction and then allows the child 'wait time'. The teacher notices that John has chosen not to begin his science work. She approaches non-threateningly and says:

*John, start work on your science please.*

The teacher then walks away communicating an expectation of compliance and allowing John 'wait time'. She uses this time to acknowledge children who are behaving appropriately.

The teacher makes sure she unobtrusively watches for any move John makes towards compliance and quickly acknowledges it.

## Step 5 - Acknowledge and redirect.

The teacher acknowledges the child's response to the instruction/direction and then *redirects* instead of arguing.

The teacher, aware that Joan chose not to respond to her initial direction says:
*Joan, start work on your science please.*

Joan responds argumentatively:
*I don't feel like it.*

The teacher chooses to redirect instead of arguing and replies:
*Joan, I understand that you don't feel like it and we can talk about that after the lesson, but right now I want you start work on your science please.*

**The teacher chooses to redirect instead of arguing...**

The teacher gives 'wait time' and scans for the opportunity to acknowledge any move Joan makes towards compliance.

### Step 6 - Rule reminder.

The teacher gives a private, assertive rule reminder.

Scanning the classroom, the teacher becomes aware that Paul has not responded to her redirection. He is still wasting time sharpening his pencil so, as calmly and as privately as she can, she reminds Paul of the class rule.

*Paul our rule for working during science is (..........). Do that now, please.*

The teacher gives Paul 'wait time' and scans for any move towards compliance.

### Step 7 - Offer a choice.

The teacher makes the consequences of inappropriate behaviour clear via offering a choice. The teacher notices that Geoff has chosen to ignore the rule reminder and is still out of his seat and disrupting a nearby group. She says:

*Geoff, you can choose to start work now or (........), thanks.*

The teacher gives 'wait time' and scans for any move towards compliance.

### Step 8 - 'Cool Off'.

The teacher directs the student to work away from others to 'cool off'.

The teacher is aware that Jane has chosen not to respond to the less invasive strategies and has refused to begin her work, so, as privately as she can, she approaches Jane and says:

**...as privately as she can, she approaches Jane...**

*Jane, I can see you've chosen to work away from the others for 5 minutes. Go now, please.*

After Jane has completed her cooling off period, the teacher says:
*Jane, thanks for doing your cool-off time. When you are ready you can rejoin the class, come back to your desk and try again.*

## Step 9 - Exit plan.

When other children are not able to learn, the teacher is not able to teach and the classroom is significantly disrupted, then a teacher may have to 'exit' a student. An exit plan is the *most intrusive action* a teacher can take and must be preceded by steps aimed at helping the children manage their own behaviour in the classroom.

The most common reasons a student may give to be exited from the classroom include:

- fighting;
- dangerous behaviour;
- tantrums that won't settle down; and
- any behaviour that continuously stops others from learning or you from teaching (not behaviour that you choose to stop and deal with).

Talented teachers do not exit children from their classrooms for throwing a tantrum or swearing just once. They rely on the techniques described in the 'big toe first' to deal with such occurrences.

Capable teachers employ their exit procedures calmly and clearly while paying a minimum of attention to inappropriate behaviour. They also let the exited child know they will be accepted back into the room as soon as they are prepared to follow the class rules.

Effective teachers are aware that if they are continually exiting a child from their room then it may indicate a problem with them as much as with the child.

**Talented teachers do not exit children from their classrooms for throwing a tantrum or swearing just once.**

**An exiting plan always contains the following points:**

- Who will actually exit the child?

  Problems occur most rapidly when the exiting is left to the classroom teacher. It is an enormously difficult task to exit a highly aggressive or angry child and cope with 30 other children at the same time. Some schools allocate senior staff to help exit a highly disruptive child. Some teachers team up with a colleague. Some teachers use a card and runner system to alert administration of the need for assistance in exiting the child.

- **Where** will the exited student go?

  - Will it be a time-out room?
  - Will it be to the coordinator's/deputy's room?

- **What** will happen to the exited student?

  - Will parents be notified?
  - Will 'counselling' take place?

- **When** will the student return to his/her class.

  - After completing 'time-out'?
  - After completing a behaviour contract?
  - After verbally agreeing to abide by the classroom rules?

- **What** will happen if the child chooses to break rules again?

These questions then form the building blocks of a respectful exiting plan. They are complemented by a teacher's attention to appropriate behaviour, his/her sense of humour and a realisation that although you can not control children's behaviour, you can provide an environment where socially appropriate behaviours can be developed and supported.

The 'big toe first' technique unfolds an unhurried and gently assertive way. Each step is built on the one before it. It is the *ultimate* strategy for keeping classrooms in the temperate zone  There are, however, other strategies that you can use to great effect.

**SUMMARY**

- Effective teachers never deal with challenging behaviour by jumping off the deep end. They test the waters with their 'big toe first' and wade quietly and unobtrusively from the shallows to help manage classroom disruptions.

- Unless a class is severely interrupted, teachers need to do a lot of wading before exiting a child.

# CHAPTER 6

## Choice-Driven Teaching

**...effective teachers are able to carry their own emotional climate with them.**

Depending on your personality, you'll find that different behaviours exhibited by different children have a different effect on your emotional climate. Effective teachers have developed and practised a remarkable ability to remain 'unflappably' calm, even amidst the most testing of situations. It seems that as much as some children try to move the classroom into the **torrid** zone, effective teachers are able to carry their own emotional climate with them. Whether it rains or shines makes no difference to them. *Their behaviour is not a function of the emotional weather — they are choice-driven.*

Through exercising this 'freedom of choice', accomplished teachers are able to **choose** their response to a situation. The response they choose is always the one that is best suited to **keeping the climate temperate** in the classroom system.

### THE CHOICE-DRIVEN MODEL

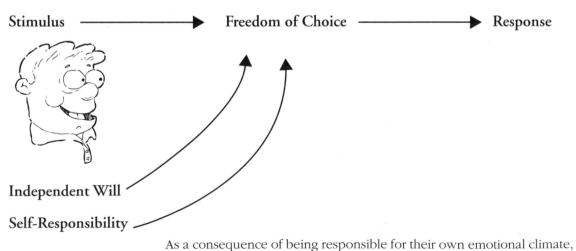

Stimulus ⟶ Freedom of Choice ⟶ Response

Independent Will

Self-Responsibility

As a consequence of being responsible for their own emotional climate, skilful teachers are not easily sidetracked from their primary behavioural goals **(PBG)**.

They **refuse** to be distracted by secondary, relatively unimportant issues, issues that achieve little else besides making everyone sweat.

Reactive teachers on the other hand ARE affected by the current emotional climate. When children behave inappropriately they become *aggressive/ defensive/protective* and slip easily into a game of, *You forced me to make the room hot* with their class.

Too many times such teachers set out to achieve an objective only to be deflected from their original goal by children. Children are past masters at pushing emotional buttons, laying red herrings, throwing false trails and otherwise getting teachers cleverly enmeshed in secondary issues.

**Children are past masters at pushing emotional buttons...**

The teacher, whose goal is to get John to put his marbles in a bag, offers John a choice at Step 7 of the 'big toe first' strategy.

*John, you can either put those marbles in your bag, which means you'll be able to use them at lunchtime, or on my desk, which means you'll have to come and get them after school.*

The teacher returns to pay attention to appropriate behaviour, thus giving wait time and keeps an eye open for compliance.

John, grumbling and mumbling all the way drops his marbles in his bag with a clatter.

*I'll put them in my bag, all right?!*

The teacher, not being sidetracked by the secondary issues of grumbling, moaning and clattering, sticks to her PBG and says:

*Thanks for doing that, John.*

Of course, there are 'traditional' ways that children endeavour to embroil teachers in a game of 'let's get torrid'. They're easily identified by that 'gut reaction' you feel in the pit of your stomach.

**Effective teachers give themselves 'wait time' to make sure they don't follow their 'gut reaction' because they know their gut reaction is what the child is after.**

Effective teachers give themselves 'wait time' to make sure they don't follow their 'gut reaction' because they know their gut reaction is what the child is after.

'Fight with me!' is a game that Ronald likes to play with his teachers.

The teacher who is at Step 6 of the 'big toe first' strategy and whose primary goal is get Ronald to begin work, says:

*Ronald, put that comic book away and start work on your science, please.*

The teacher gives Ronald 'wait time' and looks for compliance.

Ronald, in a high pitched whining voice, complains:

*I don't like science. I'm doing this (reading comic). You're always picking on me.*

By doing this, he is inviting the teacher to fight and get involved in secondary issues.

The teacher gives herself wait time to get

over her gut reaction and sticks to her PBG.

*I understand that you don't like science (acknowledges child) and we can talk about that later, but right now I want you to put the comic away and begin science. Thanks (redirects).*

The teacher gives Ronald 'wait time' and looks for compliance.

Ronald bangs his comic in his desk but **begins to work**.

The teacher, **recognising she has achieved her PBG** chooses to ignore the banging (secondary issues) and acknowledges Ronald's cooperation with a 'thumbs-up' signal as she catches his eye.

What Ronald's teacher did is what all highly effective teachers do and that's to give herself 'wait time' and thereby exercise her **freedom of choice** to keep the class in the temperate zone.

Some of the key (O▬═) ways that **you** can exercise your freedom of choice to keep it temperate in your classroom are:

O▬═ Always use a respectful voice when dealing with a child. This means no shouting or yelling.

The teacher who is at step 5 of the 'big toe first' strategy keeps her voice assertive yet well-modulated.

*Mark, leave the computer and come back to your desk please.*

The teacher gives wait time and looks for compliance.

O━☰ Avoid using sarcasm, emotionally-loaded language or humour that is belittling to another person.

**You can use humour that is self-defacing as children tend to love it.**

You can use humour that is self-defacing as children tend to love it. The teacher, making a mental maths error says:

*Course, you know what I'm like, about as smart as a door jamb — on a good day.*

O━☰ Always use respectful body language that allows the child to maintain dignity and 'save face'.

Unless you want to play a game of 'fight with me' avoid:
• thrusting and wagging your finger;
• fast 'front on' approaches;
• invading personal space; and
• backing a child into a corner either physically or emotionally.

Compare these two scenarios.

1. The teacher, walking quickly towards child, hands on hips leaning forward at the waist, thrusts her face into the child's personal space and says in a loud threatening voice:

   *How many times have I told you to start work, son?*

2. The teacher, approaching the child from the side, lowers to the child's level, avoiding invading the child's personal space, and says:

   *Mary, can I help you with that maths problem?*

O━☰ Always talk about the child's behaviour as being unacceptable

**(not the child).** There's a big difference between,

*Mark you're a bully,* and

*Mark, hitting others is completely unacceptable.*

Remember, **HYPNOSIS IS AN EVERYDAY EVENT** and if children hear you constantly giving them a label like 'troublemaker' they will endeavour to live down to it.

O━━▇ Deal with problems in private and avoid public reprimands as they can be viewed as an opportunity to fight.

**Deal with problems in private and avoid public reprimands...**

The duty teacher spots a child dropping a piece of rubbish in the playground with a group of friends and says:

*Jeff, may I see you for a second, please?*

Jeff moves away from group influence and the need to 'save face'.

*Jeff, just pop that rubbish in the bin please. Thanks.*

The duty teacher gives 'wait time' and
leaves communicating expectation of compliance.
Jeff chooses to comply and the teacher acknowledges
Jeff with a smile and a wink.

O━━▇ If a game of 'lets get torrid' does eventuate and the class moves into the 'torrid zone', successful teachers never wait for the child to apologise or humble themselves before making a positive approach; they always make the first move.

When Josh has had a two minute 'cool-off' period, the teacher chooses to make the first positive move and says:

*Josh, thanks for doing your cool-off. Come back to your seat and try again. Call me if you need some help.*

By exercising their freedom of choice and choosing the best response to keep the classroom 'temperate', resourceful teachers not only keep their classrooms out of the 'torrid zone' but also help to establish with their children healthy 'emotional gardens'.

## SUMMARY

- You have choice. You are not driven by your surroundings but by personal choice.
- Personal choice is your most powerful tool in the classroom. It is the ultimate way to keep the classroom tone temperate.
- By being choice-driven instead of reactionary you will find you can stick to your PBG which will help make you a more effective teacher.

# CHAPTER 7

# Emotional Gardening

I t is precisely because effective teachers are not magicians that the best effects of the tactics they use are not always obvious. Although many of their strategies are immediately effective in managing challenging behaviour, their real success lies in the cumulative daily effect of the **choice-driven** relationships they have with children.

The term 'emotional gardening' is a useful metaphor for describing how highly able teachers develop rapport and trust with a child or with a class.

'The greatest thing by far is to be master of a metaphor.'
...Aristotle.

Anyone who has nurtured a regular garden already understands how an 'emotional garden' works. Individuals who initially take the time on a daily basis to tend to their regular gardens soon find that they become established and demand less care and attention. A healthy and well-established garden can also stand much of nature's harsh treatment without undue damage. Teachers who initially take the time on a daily basis to tend to their 'emotional gardens' soon find that their garden

becomes well-established. You feed and tend an 'emotional garden' just as you would a regular garden. With care and love the seeds of rapport and trust will thrive, blossom and grow. Teachers who have a healthy and well-established 'emotional garden' also find that it can weather many of the storms that can occur in the classroom without undue damage. Just as a regular garden can repay you for your time and effort with its blossoms and fruits, so an emotional garden can repay you many times over for your time and effort. Avid emotional gardeners regularly find the fruits of their labour are children who are cooperative, easy to get along with, open to suggestions and forgiving of their blunders.

Resourceful teachers, because of their choice-driven behaviour and as a result of keeping their classrooms in the temperate zone, consistently tend to their 'emotional gardens' and over time are blessed with bountiful returns.

## Guaranteed ways you can make gains with your children's emotional garden

**0━═ Consistently follow the strategies already suggested in this book:**

- the 'greens and sandtraps' strategy;
- the 'big toe first' technique;
- 'choice-driven' teaching;
- the 'BBQ' technique;
- acting 'as if';
- using the 'inside-out approach' to change; and
- using a model of teaching based on influence and not control.

**0━═ Take the time to understand each child.**

Remember that children are individuals and have individual needs and wants. Not all children see school as a positive experience and teachers as nurturing individuals. In fact, some of the more difficult children in your class will have developed a belief system that causes them to 'see' your actions in a very different light from the way you 'see' them. For example, some children thrive on public praise whereas others find it unbearably embarrassing.

**...children who are cooperative, easy to get along with, open to suggestions and forgiving of their blunders.**

**Not all children see school as a positive experience and teachers as nurturing individuals.**

**O═ Concentrate on the little things.**

Small, consistent acts of courtesy and respect help to quickly establish and maintain a bountiful emotional garden. Many of us feel that we're just too busy for the 'small stuff' and yet it's the teachers who do manage to pay attention to the small stuff who have the healthiest gardens. A teacher who notices children cooperating or a small improvement in handwriting is the sort of teacher whose nurturing attention to the little things will end up paying big dividends.

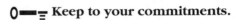

**O═ Keep to your commitments.**

Trust is built through keeping to your commitments. The biggest break in trust is caused by committing yourself to a respectful management plan and then not following through.

**O═ Present a practical learning environment.**

Have a room that is set up for children and not just for teachers and inspectors.

**O═ Cater and plan for mixed abilities.**

One of the clearest messages behind behaviour is, 'This is too hard/ easy for me'. As much as possible, plan for interesting lessons that utilise appropriate materials.

**O═ Be punctual.**

Preventative action means that you won't arrive late at your classroom to find it in an uproar.

**O═ Avoid using labels when you deal with children.**

Labels are demeaning and simply attach meanings that we assign to other human beings.

### ○━≡ Never be duplicitous.

- Don't make 'throw away' comments about a child when talking to others.
- Don't say one thing to a child and another to his/her parents.
- Under no circumstances gossip about a child or his/her family.

### ○━≡ Apologise sincerely if you make a mistake.

Make sure you apologise if you treat someone badly or make an error of judgment. Apologies take great strength of character and children respect that.

### ○━≡ Teach your children the classroom routines.

A terrific way to tend to your emotional garden on a daily basis is to teach your children the 'what if' routines.

- What to do if you want to go to the toilet.
- What to do if your pen runs out.
- What to do if you can't spell a word.
- What to do if you've left your homework at home.
- What to do if you finish work early.

Consider these two scenarios.

1. A teacher, who has not specifically taught the 'what if' routines, is busy working with a group of children on the mat. She is interrupted by Ben and communicating her annoyance says,
   *Ben, go and find something to do until I've finished.*

2. A teacher, who has specifically taught the 'what if' routines, is busy working on the mat with a group of children. She notices Ben has finished and, reinforcing appropriate classroom behaviour, says:
   *Ben, great to see you know what to do when you've finished your reading.*

In this way she not only acknowledges appropriate behaviour but also tends to her emotional garden. There are many routines and if you teach your children a variety of them, you provide yourself with a great opportunity to reinforce appropriate behaviour. They also help you create the conditions under which the seeds of success can grow.

## O━₌ Re-establish working relationships as soon as possible.

As the teacher moves around the room she is aware that Jared is using the science equipment inappropriately to amuse (and disrupt) the group with which he is working. She uses the 'big toe first' technique but at each step Jared chooses to continue his disruptive behaviour. As the 'big toe first' technique gently unfolds with Jared, the teacher is constantly scanning the rest of the class and acknowledging appropriate behaviour. Eventually she approaches Jared and says:

*Jared, I can see you've chosen 5 minutes cool-off time away from your group. Go now, please.*

As soon as Jared's 5 minutes cool-off time are up, the teacher makes the first positive move and says:

*Jared, thanks for doing your cool-off time. Come back to your desk and try again.*

As soon as the teacher notices Jared behaving appropriately (or approximating appropriate behaviour), she takes the opportunity to re-establish a working relationship with him. She might say something like:

*Thanks for starting work on your science, Jared. You look like you're making good progress.*
or,

*Terrific, Jared, you've started. Let me know if you need any help.*

or,

*It's fantastic to see you settle down so quickly, Jared. I'd love to see how your experiment turns out.*

**A healthy 'emotional garden' is developed on a daily basis through small, often unnoticed acts. Though their effects may not be felt for weeks or even months, effective teachers can be seen enjoying the fruits of their labour in classrooms everywhere.**

A healthy 'emotional garden' is developed on a daily basis through small, often unnoticed acts. Though their effects may not be felt for weeks or even months, effective teachers can be seen enjoying the fruits of their labour in classrooms everywhere.

Trust, rapport and mutual respect are the bounties available to teachers who take the time to establish and maintain a healthy 'emotional garden'.

Every talented teacher I know has green thumbs. You should, too.

## SUMMARY

- Highly effective teachers are not magicians and the best effects of the strategies they use are not always obvious.
- Emotional gardening is a great way to build trust and rapport with children.
- Teachers who take the time to nurture their 'emotional gardens' find the effort well worthwhile.

# CHAPTER 8

# Punishment

One of the most polarising issues in teaching today is the issue of PUNISHMENT. To punish or not to punish? That is the question. There are renewed calls for the return of corporal punishment from some sections of the teaching fraternity who feel they have been let down by 'the system'. They feel the authority that teachers traditionally had has been undermined by a bunch of 'do-gooders'.

*Our hands are tied. Without a viable method of punishing children, how do you expect us to control them?* they ask.

However, a **Brilliantly Better Question** to ask is, *Even with their 'hands tied', how do resourceful teachers somehow manage to reinforce clear and consistent boundaries to acceptable behaviour?*

As with most other aspects of complex systems management there is no simple answer to this question. There are, however, many clues which lie in the fundamentally different way some teachers view the concept of punishment in their classroom.

They use to their advantage the notions of:

1. *Formal as opposed to informal management;*

2. *The language of self-responsibility as opposed to the language of control;*

3. *Consequence 'loops' as opposed to escalating severity;*

4. *Feedback as opposed to mistakes; and*

5. *Forgiveness.*

## 1. Formal as opposed to informal management.

There are two types of management strategies teachers can choose to use in schools and classes. The first is the **formal management** strategy. Formal management strategies utilise the existing power structures that define the parameters within which the school, its staff, the parents and children operate.

Examples of formal power structures are:

- Acts of parliament;
- Education Department regulations and policies;
- Occupational Health and Safety regulations; and
- School/class care and discipline policies.

Formal strategies are predictable and consistent. They refer to lines of authority, areas of responsibility and codes of behaviour. They reflect the causes of social justice and equal rights and are framed within nondiscriminatory boundaries. Practised teachers, by having a formal care and discipline plan, choose to trap and use these formal power structures to the mutual advantage of the children, the teachers, the administrators and the parents in the school community.

Formal management strategies are written down and are available for everyone to see. They are therefore more likely to be predictable and consistent and predictability and consistency are two of the cornerstones of effective behaviour management.

**...predictability and consistency are two of the cornerstones of effective behaviour management.**

**Informal management** strategies are not so clearly delineated and include:

- Age - I'm an adult, don't argue with me;
- Gender - he needs a strong male hand;
- Emotional blackmail - anger, manipulation, pleading; and
- One-upmanship - sarcasm, public ridicule, humour at someone else's expense.

Informal power structures carry subtle hidden messages. The learnings inherent in these hidden messages can cause teachers conflict in the classroom.

Some of the hidden learnings for children are:

- 'Unpredictability' is the norm. If the teacher has a problem, everyone has a problem, so you had better be darn good at playing, 'Find out what mood the teacher is in';
- My behaviour is not my responsibility. If the teacher did his/her job properly and used the right informal management strategy (shouting at me) I'd behave — for a little while anyway;
- The best way to beat the system is by getting better at playing the system's own game (e.g. If I'm sulky enough or angry enough I'll get what I want);
- Power and authority come from above not from within; and
- The best way of handling people is through informal power structures.

Informal management strategies, because of their inconsistency, often invite children to think of creative ways to avoid being punished. Punishment is an informal method of management in that it is at the discretion of the punisher when punishment is seen to be appropriate and what type of punishment is seen to be suitable. Punishers deal with misbehaviour **as they see fit.**

**Punishers deal with misbehaviour as they see fit.**

## 2. The language of self-responsibility as opposed to the language of control.

Capable teachers understand that children learn most rapidly when they have a genuine sense of responsibility for their actions. If we know our fate is in our own hands, then learning matters.

Successful teachers use language which reflects self-responsibility for behaviour in their classrooms. They verbalise clearly for children exactly who is responsible for choosing to behave inappropriately. Consider Chris's teacher, who is at Step 7 of the 'big toe first' strategy, and whose aim is to help Chris understand that he is responsible for his own behaviour. She says:

*Chris, I can see that **you have chosen** to sit away from the class for 2 minutes. Go now, please.*

The focus is on helping children understand they are responsible for and must accept the consequences of their own behaviour. Effective teachers understand when children are faced with accepting responsibility for their own behaviour the locus of control lies clearly with them — as it should.

This is in direct contrast to the teacher who says:

*Right, that's it Chris, I can't stand your interruptions a moment longer— I want you out of my room and don't come back until you've changed your attitude to school.*

## 3. The consequence 'loop' as opposed to escalating severity.

'If you want to succeed, double your failure rate.'
…Thomas Watson, founder of IBM.

When you deal with difficult-to-manage children it soon becomes abundantly clear that increasing the severity of the consequences has very little effect on the likelihood of the inappropriate behaviour recurring. What it usually leads to instead, is a prolonged visit to the 'torrid zone' and the child spending increased amounts of time out of the classroom, which is the very environment they have to develop new bushtracks for. It's akin to trying to teach someone to swim yet always keeping them out of the water. The term 'consequence loop' was coined by a dear friend of mine, Malcolm Reed, while talking to a group of trainee teachers about classroom management. He used the term 'consequence loop' to describe how it is that effective teachers use the strategy of 'cool-off' time in their classrooms. He wanted to make it clear that the power of a consequence comes from its certainty. Malcolm's notion of a 'consequence loop' suggests that whenever possible, children be consistently 'looped' back into the classroom after experiencing the consequence of their behaviour — instead of being escalated out of the room for increasing amounts of time. A teacher might, for example, continue to 'loop' Mark back into her classroom (after he has spent 2 minutes 'cool-off' time) each time he chose not to work. Effective teachers know they increase the likelihood of 'catching' a child behaving appropriately by having the child in their room. They know they can begin to generate whole new bushtracks, options and choices for children if they can just notice and acknowledge appropriate behaviour in the class. By ensuring that children spend as much time in class as possible, skilful teachers are well on the way to creating whole new positive paths for children.

**…increasing the severity of the consequence has very little effect on the likelihood of the inappropriate behaviour recurring.**

**Effective teachers know they increase the likelihood of 'catching' a child behaving appropriately by having the child in their room.**

## 4. Mistakes versus feedback.

'Many people dream of success. To me success can only be achieved through repeated failure and introspection.'
...Soichiro Honda, founder of Honda Motors.

Children learn most effectively when they receive feedback about the action they have taken. Feedback is vital to any learning environment, and another word for feedback is 'mistake'.

Effective teachers embrace feedback as one of the most important learning opportunities children can have. They are pleased to allow children to experience feedback about their behaviour.

**Action**  ▶▶ **Feedback**  ▶▶ **Learning**  ▶▶ **New Action**

'How often I saw where I should be going by arriving in the wrong place.'
...Buckminster Fuller.

'Effective behaviour managers use the term 'consequence' rather than 'punishment' when they are talking about inappropriate behaviour. They take the view that consequences are the perfect way for children to learn and therefore to adjust their behaviour. Consequences are never used as a threat and are always expressed as the child's own choice.

**Consequences are never used as a threat and are always expressed as the child's own choice.**

82

*Consequences* are like aikido, which aims to use an opponent's own force against him. There is no resistance or struggle, no effort to control. There is just a fluidity experienced by the attacker as he is allowed to feel the results of his own unleashing of power.

Punishment on the other hand is like karate. It meets force with force. It aims to overcome through superior firepower and is often met with powerful resistance. Effective teachers understand that children need to learn in an environment where they are free to make mistakes. They understand that if you can not make mistakes you can not learn.

'I am never afraid to make a mistake.'
…Michael Jordan.

## 5. Forgiveness.

To encourage learning through mistakes (feedback) is to allow, and perhaps even to encourage, risk taking. But to encourage risk taking you must be prepared to practise forgiveness. Real forgiveness is to forgive and to forget. Real forgiveness includes reconciliation. Children must never come to believe they have used up their final chance. The best teachers know this and in their classrooms you can hear them say, *Chris, thanks for doing your time-out. You can come back to your desk and **try again.***

**But to encourage risk taking you must be prepared to practise forgiveness.**

Highly skilled teachers set in motion a powerful set of circumstances that allow children to learn in the most natural way that:

- all behaviour has consequences; and
- responsibility for behaviour must be owned.

If you've ever watched a child learn a new skill you'll be aware of how quickly he/she can learn in an environment free of fear where feedback results in changed behaviour. Children learn to behave in the classroom in much the same way.

**SUMMARY**

- The issue of punishment is a particularly hoary one and any discussion on the topic is sure to be lively.
- To create clear boundaries between acceptable and unacceptable behaviour, you can:
  1. Have a formal care and discipline policy;
  2. Plan for ways to let children hear they are responsible for their behaviour;
  3. Be consistent, consistent, consistent rather than increasingly harsh;
  4. Think of mistakes as feedback; and
  5. Practise real forgiveness.

# CHAPTER 9

# Rewards

I was giving a presentation to a group of postgraduate students at a teacher training institution in England, talking about the importance of rewards in the classroom, when a lecturer jumped to his feet and accused me of ruining the youth of today. He claimed that by encouraging trainee teachers to 'bribe' children into being good in the classroom I was going to help create a generation of adults who would only work, and I quote, *if there was something in it for them.*

It's not the first time I've been accused of such heresy, as there are a number of teachers who feel that 'bribery' will be the ruin of many a poor child. Coincidentally though, I've become aware that many of these same teachers spend a good deal of their professional time applying for promotions and pay rises or looking for opportunities to increase their status or kudos. The message seems to be, 'do as I say, not as I do'. In other words, it is alright for me to seek a pay-off for what I do, but you're supposed to have an intrinsic love for the lessons I present to you (in your best interests, of course).

Contrary to this view, practised teachers work using a very basic model that states: 'people move towards situations that cause them pleasure'. Effective teachers are quite happy to use extrinsic pay-offs initially to help children move towards a positive learning situation.

**...'people move towards situations that cause them pleasure'.**

### The Intrinsic Ladder

Only when children have internalised a 'feel-good sensation' which has been linked to appropriate behaviour can they be intrinsically motivated to behave appropriately in a classroom. This internalised 'feel-good sensation' doesn't just happen through osmosis. First it has to be matched to an extrinsic reward often enough for the child to link 'feeling good' with an extrinsic reward — which itself has been paired with behaving appropriately. Each time an external pay-off which produces a 'feel-good' sensation is linked to behaving appropriately it increases the likelihood that behaving appropriately will be linked internally with feeling good. It's like a ladder leading from no link between feeling good and appropriate behaviour on the bottom rung, to a powerful link between feeling good and behaving appropriately on the top rung.

Many children come to school with a strong internal link between behaving appropriately and feeling good — many do not.

Children are individuals and individuals climb ladders at different rates. Some will race to the top quickly and, with very few trials, link feeling good and behaving appropriately. Others will be scared of heights and take many trials to link appropriate behaviour with feeling good. Effective teachers understand this and are prepared to lead the child up the ladder using the carrot instead of trying to force them up using the stick. Pay-offs for appropriate behaviour provide teachers with a tool for helping children climb the intrinsic ladder. Used correctly, pay-offs help foster a genuine team spirit in the classroom as well as helping create an environment where learning through feedback is truly valued. As with many other aspects of classroom management, highly effective teachers use reinforcement schemes in ways that can be observed and modelled. I have attempted to isolate for you those distinctions that I believe can truly make a difference to your teaching.

**Used correctly, pay-offs help foster a genuine team spirit in the classroom...**

Regardless of what sort of pay-off scheme they choose to use, skilful teachers use general guidelines to help children link behaving appropriately in the classroom with that 'feel-good' sensation. They:

1. ***Reward appropriate behaviour as soon as possible;***
2. ***Make the pay-offs small and attainable;***
3. ***Make the rewards cumulative;***
4. ***Make the pay-offs cooperative;***
5. ***Never take back a reward;***
6. ***Use the element of pleasant expectation; and***
7. ***Avoid the 'hidden negatives'.***

## 1. They reward appropriate behaviour as soon as possible.

If they are using points on a chart, then the chart is always within reach. If they are using raffle tickets, then they always have a pocketful handy. I call it the 'Wyatt Earp' syndrome. Effective teachers are fast on the draw and they reinforce appropriate behaviour quickly so the moment is still fresh. Compare these two scenarios.

**Effective teachers are fast on the draw and they reinforce appropriate behaviour quickly…**

**a.** The music teacher who has just taken a very successful lesson, leads the year fours back to their home room, sits them down and says: *Mark, you listened well at the beginning of the lesson, here's a class point. Lisa, when we were playing our recorder you concentrated hard, here's a class point for you. Joel, you walked back to the classroom sensibly, here's a class point for you.*

This teacher has obviously attempted to reinforce appropriate behaviour but the moment has died.

The link between the appropriate behaviour and the reward becomes more tenuous as time passes.

Follow now as a practised behaviour manager rewards positive classroom behaviour.

**b.** The music teacher, who is taking a very successful lesson, spots Mark listening carefully and says, *Mark, thanks for listening carefully,* and hands him a class point. During the lesson she notices Lisa concentrating and says, *Lisa, it's terrific to see you concentrating. Here is a class point.*

In this classroom there is a strong link between the reward and the appropriate behaviour. Try strapping on your six guns and noticing the effect the 'Wyatt Earp' strategy has on your classroom.

**...children don't experience time the same way an adult does.**

### 2. They make the pay-offs small but attainable.

Successful behaviour managers understand that children don't experience time the same way an adult does. A week is a very long time in a young child's life—an especially long time to wait for a pay-off. As a general guideline, five-and six-year-olds need a pay-off every couple of days. Seven-and eight-year-olds need a pay-off every three to four days. Nine-and ten-year-olds need a pay-off every five to six days. Eleven-and twelve-year-olds should be receiving a pay-off in about eight days and teenagers shouldn't be kept waiting any longer than about twelve days for a pay-off.

Unlike successful behaviour managers, some teachers try to 'bleed' their reinforcement scheme for as much time as possible, often as much as a whole term. The logic behind this is quite clear *once you're aware of the pay-offs these teachers are offering children.* Most are far too extravagant and because they are so extravagant the teachers feel that they need to get their money's worth. They feel that the best way to get their money's worth is to stretch out the pay-off's 'use by' date for as long as possible. Effective teachers are aware that the adage 'a little and often' works well as a general rule of thumb in regards to pay-offs for children. Because children are receiving their pay-offs fairly regularly, a pay-off can be as little as a 15-minute popcorn party or 15 minutes viewing time of a favourite video or......(you're only limited by your own imagination).

...'a little and often'...

## 3. They make the pay-offs cumulative.

When I first began to integrate very difficult children back into regular classrooms I learned a lot about the value of making pay-offs cumulative. I remember clearly one particular incident with Dan. Dan had been attending a withdrawal centre for behaviourally disturbed children for 18 months and part of my job was to get him back into mainstream classes. Initially I tried saying to Dan's teacher, *Between morning recess and lunchtime there are nine 10-minute intervals. If Dan is behaving appropriately* (he had a contract to define 'behaving appropriately') *during a 10-minute interval he earns a token for that period. If he can earn six out of the nine possible tokens then he earns his pay-off.'*

Well, Dan came to school in one heck of a foul mood that first day and didn't earn his first token. In fact he didn't earn his first four tokens. Now, Dan was a behaviour problem but he wasn't stupid and it took him about one microsecond to realise he could no longer earn his pay-off. Dan now saw himself as having nothing left to lose and his poor behaviour escalated fairly rapidly.

After lots of talking, the classroom teacher and I realised that we could help provide Dan with the right setting in which he could develop new bushtracks with a simple change of perspective. We said to Dan, *When you earn six tokens you have earned a pay-off, you take as long as you want to do that* (locus of control is Dan's).

It didn't matter whether Dan had a bad session or not because he was always working towards something. After a hiccup we would say to him, *Dan, only (three) tokens to go before your pay-off.*

Accomplished teachers use this same strategy with the children in their class. Instead of saying to the children, ***If*** *you can fill this jar with marbles by Friday you've earned your pay-off,* they say, ***When*** *this jar is full of marbles, you have earned your pay-off — I think you can do it by Friday.*

**Effective teachers always set their children and themselves up for success by using pay-offs that are cumulative in their classrooms.**

Effective teachers always set their children and themselves up for success by using pay-offs that are cumulative in their classrooms.

### 4. They make the pay-offs cooperative.

Whenever they can, highly competent teachers foster a working environment that is cooperative rather than competitive. One sure way they can foster a cooperative working environment is to have a pay-off system from which everyone benefits. As a classroom teacher you have a choice as to whether an individual child, a group or the whole class will benefit from a pay-off. Effective teachers always choose to use a whole-class pay-off scheme to foster cooperation in their rooms. They set up a situation where each child is working cooperatively towards a pay-off for the whole class. Everyone is a winner and everyone is motivated to help their classmates behave appropriately.

With pay-offs that can only be won by individuals or individual groups there must be losers (probably more losers than winners). To be a winner it must be at the expense of those who lose. So it is in the winners' best interests to have others who don't know how to win, and not to help them learn how. Unwittingly, we set up some children or groups of children in our classrooms for failure because it's in some children's best interests to keep others from learning how to behave.

**Unwittingly, we set some children or groups of children in our classrooms up for failure...**

## Star of the Day

An excellent strategy I've seen used in classrooms to help foster a cooperative learning environment is called the 'Star for the day'. It works like this.

First, the teacher makes up two or three badges that have a star or a smiling face on them. Next, with a great deal of ceremony, the teacher informs the class that at the beginning of each morning he/she will select two or three children who will be chosen to wear the star for the day badges. These badges, he/she tells the class, mean that the teacher will be looking very carefully for every opportunity to notice and reward appropriate behaviour in the wearer. Not only that, whenever the 'star for the day' is noticed behaving appropriately he/she earns double or triple the number of points anybody else would earn — **for the class.**

The rest of the class now has a real investment in seeing that the star for the day is 'caught' behaving well as often as possible. Individual encouragement and support for the star of the day becomes a valid strategy for earning a pay-off for the whole class. Masterful teachers are aware that the 'star for the day' badge is also a tool that helps them focus on and reinforce appropriate behaviour in children. Try this strategy on for size and you'll notice how it changes your perspective to assist you to look for and find even the most difficult children behaving appropriately.

### 5. They never take back a reward.

…never rub out the stamp, take a marble out of the jar, a raffle ticket off the desk or remove a point from the chart.

Effective teachers never take back or threaten to take back a pay-off once it is earned. They never rub out the stamp, take a marble out of the jar, a raffle ticket off the desk or remove a point from the chart. Instead, they help children to learn from the results of their choices/actions by allowing them to experience the formally agreed upon class consequence for inappropriate behaviour.  Compare these two teachers.

a. The first teacher, after just reinforcing three children for sitting quietly and working, notices that one of the children is stopping the person next to him from working. She says, *Sam, what do you think you're doing? I just gave you a class star for working. Well, you've just lost that one!*

b. The second teacher, in the same situation, says, *Sam, I can see that you have chosen to sit quietly by yourself for two minutes. Go now, please.*

### 6. They use the element of pleasant surprise.

…this state of pleasant surprise is a very motivating state in which to be.

You don't have to be in a practised teacher's room long to realise that constantly used strategies are in place that keep the children in a state of pleasant surprise and this state of pleasant surprise is a very **motivating** state in which to be. I call three of their favourite strategies for keeping children in a state of pleasant surprise the 'jackpot', the 'freebie' and the 'chameleon'.

#### The 'jackpot'

Every now and then, and quite unpredictably, effective teachers 'jackpot' the expected pay-off for a child. Consider Mark's teacher, who has noticed him working sensibly on the word processor and says, *Mark, thanks for working quietly on the word processor. You've just earned two points for the class chart.* Now, Mark is only expecting one and is pleased and surprised to receive two. (So are his classmates.) This element of pleasant surprise doesn't leave Mark quickly, however, because he can't help contemplating the fact that this *unexpected* and *unpredictable* pay-off might occur again. Mark's teacher has put Mark in a state of pleasant human surprise and this is a highly motivating state for Mark to be in.

### The 'freebie'

I'm sure the 'freebie' is a strategy that effective teachers have borrowed from animal trainers. If you watch animal trainers work you notice they occasionally 'reward' the animals they are training for no apparent reason whatsoever. If you ask the animal trainer why they've rewarded the animal for no apparent reason they reply, 'To make the animal feel good because animals that feel good are more likely to give you what you want'.

Children will react in the same way. Children who feel good are more likely to give you what you want. Able behaviour managers take advantage of this fact and every now and then they will 'reward' a child for no apparent reason. An effective teacher might say, *Linda you have 10 minutes free time on the computer* and not even try to link the pay-off to behaving appropriately in the classroom. They know that this strategy has long-term benefits because it creates an environment that is conducive to cooperation between the teacher and the children.

**Children who feel good are more likely to give you what you want.**

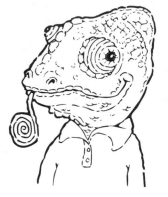

### The 'chameleon'

Effective teachers are chameleon-like in their approach to pay-off schemes. I never cease to be amazed at the number of different ways they find for varying their pay-off scheme. One week they're using marbles in the jar, the next they're using raffle tickets or a token economy or endless variations on the themes we've discussed. The point is, the children are always kept in a state of pleasant surprise and are never allowed to become blasé about the 'same old, same old'.

### 7. They avoid the hidden negatives.

Some of the pay-off schemes we set up for children end up being more negative than positive. An example is the school that decided to give all the children who had behaved appropriately in the playground for a term a special sausage sizzle as a pay-off. At first viewing this seems an altogether positive and commendable strategy to use. But what about John, who on the first day of term runs instead of walks and is given a yellow slip by the duty teacher? He experiences the consequences of his actions but then has to face up to the hidden negative — not being able to attend the sausage sizzle, for something he did on the first day of term and has probably forgotten all about. Instead of being doubly positive the scheme is loaded with a hidden negative.

I remember a teacher who used a strategy called 'musical rubbish' to help her manage her classroom. Basically what happened was the first child in the class to behave inappropriately was ordered to pick up five pieces of rubbish at the next break. The next child who behaved inappropriately inherited those five pieces of rubbish plus five more making a total of 10 pieces of rubbish. Any further child who behaved inappropriately added five more pieces to the previous total and became responsible for its collection at break time. The children thought this was great fun. They would deliberately misbehave for the first four-fifths of the lesson, pushing the rubbish collection total to new time highs, then wait for the last poor sucker to 'cop the lot' with about 20 minutes to go before the break. A strategy originally intended to limit inappropriate behaviour actually ended up encouraging it.

Effective teachers search for hidden negatives in their pay-off schemes.

## SUMMARY

- Some teachers have no time for rewards. (Rewards will 'spoil' kids anyway.)
- Other teachers use rewards effectively in their classrooms.
- Effective rewards are:

    1. Immediate;

    2. Small but attainable;

    3. Cumulative;

    4. Cooperative; and

    5. Pleasantly surprising.

# CHAPTER 10

## Putting it into Practise

**There is no genetically-endowed trait or hidden luck involved in being a highly capable behaviour manager.**

The biggest roadblock to managing challenging children successfully is the mistaken belief that teachers who are doing it well are either born with an innate gift or are perhaps just plain lucky. You need to know right here and now that it's neither.

There is no genetically-endowed trait or hidden luck involved in being a highly capable behaviour manager. Luck is something we create for ourselves; it is not due to the exterior universe. I think there are many teachers out there whom we call lucky, but who just pay better attention.

**Great teachers have great strategies and great strategies can be modelled.**

*WARNING:* Just reading this book of great strategies does not make you a great behaviour manager. Having the information is not the same as having the skill. In times of war, armies have suffered great losses due to being ambushed effectively. Soldiers under attack would instinctively do what any human being would do under similar circumstances, turn their backs to the enemy and try to get away. Unfortunately, this would make them even easier targets and the losses would be even greater. To remedy this situation, soldiers were told that in times of ambush the best defence is to face

the enemy and charge towards them, firing. At least you increase your chances of getting them before they get you. However, even though they were armed with this information, soldiers who were ambushed behaved in exactly the same way as they had done before.

In the 'heat of the moment', information is forgotten and it's the skill that will save your life.

Skills take practice. Having the information is not the same as having the skill.

**Having the information is not the same as having the skill.**

A perfect example is the first time you're silly enough to try to stand up on skis. Everyone advises you, 'lean forward' and even though you have this information, as soon as the skis begin to move forward you instinctively lean back. No one can teach you a skill and you can't get a skill from a book!

**No one can teach you a skill and you can't get a skill from a book!**

Talented behaviour managers display carefully honed and practised skills. The royal road to effective behaviour management is paved with practice.

At the core of effective teachers' finely honed skills is the realisation that *a plan* provides them with the major scaffolding upon which processes can be hung. *A care and discipline plan is always there to provide you with the confidence and 'back-up' you need when you're in the thick of things, being ambushed from all sides.*

Remember, whenever you fail to plan, you're planning to fail. I was quick to learn that in highly functional classrooms a planned approach to care and discipline means a lot more than knowing what to do when some children begin to be 'naughty'. Why is it that excellent behaviour managers seem to do things in a 'back-to-front' way?

**...whenever you fail to plan, you're planning to fail.**

In order of priority, a planned approach to care and discipline means:

- planning for positive, appropriate classroom behaviour;
- planning for how you (the teacher) are going to behave when you are inevitably confronted with inappropriate classroom behaviour; and
- planning for the creation/maintenance of new appropriate classroom behaviours.

My grandmother used to paraphrase Robbie Burns to me whenever she felt I needed guidance during my moments of teenage foolishness. (I got to know Mr. Burns fairly well.)

One of the things she used to say to me was, *Oh what a gift God could give us to see ourselves as others see us.* In this quote is a clue to one of the most effective things you can do for your teaching.

### Watch yourself teach

**Arrange to videotape yourself teaching on a regular basis...**

Arrange to videotape yourself teaching on a regular basis, (you will find a way), and watch it. The feedback that you get will be extremely powerful. You will see yourself in a completely new light, suddenly aware of all the small habits and patterns you have. Start counting and tallying the number of times you say 'shhh' or 'quiet' or the number of times you put your hands on your hips and frown. Even better, count the number of times you specifically acknowledge positive classroom behaviour or the number of times you choose to keep the class in the 'temperate zone'.

bump!

your classroom, marvelling at the way you deal with — Chris,

If you want to take your learning process to the next level, find a partner on staff that you can share your videotapes with. It has to be someone that you can trust and feel completely comfortable with because you will be sharing moments of complete vulnerability.

When I watch the most proficient teachers help children learn I become acutely aware of their undeniable ability to work in an unpredictable and dynamic environment. Originally, I thought that coping with such complexity must be the result of a complicated set of strategies and techniques — I was wrong. At the heart of everything they do are a few simple but deeply held beliefs about children and learning. From these simple, deeply held beliefs emerge strategies and techniques that appear to be complex. Effective teachers generate surface complexity from deep simplicity. I didn't want this to be a book simply about surface complexity — the strategies and techniques that you can take back to the classroom to help children behave appropriately. For when you separate the strategy from the deeply held belief that underpins it, you end up with a 'disempowered' strategy, a mere bag of tricks. It would be like having a personality without the deeper and much more important character that you deserve.

**At the heart of everything they do are a few simple but deeply held beliefs about children and learning.**

The Japanese have a word that sums up beautifully the approach to teaching that I see effective teachers of challenging children employ. It is KAIZEN. Roughly translated it means:

> 'If you take care of the *process* then the *product* will take care of itself.'
> The wonderful teachers with whom I've worked concentrate on the *processes* that are outlined in this book and the *products* do, in fact, take care of themselves. My hope is that somewhere in this book there is something that appeals to the 'process' part of you, and that one day I will be lucky enough to find myself in

who sits at the back of the room and...

**SUMMARY**

- Great teachers have great strategies and great strategies can be modelled.
- Having the information is not the same as having the skill.
- Watch yourself teach—it will completely change your perspective.
- Processes are more important than product.

# CHAPTER 11

# Conclusion

C lose your eyes, take four long deep breaths. As you breathe out each time feel yourself relaxing more and more. Now think back to a time you felt really terrific. Put yourself back into that scene, relive the experience as if you were there. Hear the sounds, see the sights, feel the feelings. Take a moment to reflect on that time.

Now, if we had instruments that were sensitive enough we would have been able to measure your physiological responses to your 'imagined event'. We would have been able to measure changes in heart rate, blood pressure and skin temperature. Some of you would have even felt emotionally excited. In engaging in this short activity you have just demonstrated a major premise underlying this book - that your body, mind and emotions interact with each other and influence your effectiveness in the classroom.

Dr. Dennis Waitley, a motivational psychologist who has worked with peak performing individuals in all walks of life and was the consulting psychologist for the Apollo program, makes it clear the traits that characterise peak performers are mental and emotional not physical or tactical.

**...traits that characterise peak performers are mental and emotional...**

After spending a great deal of time watching highly effective teachers work I believe their success in managing challenging behaviour in the classroom is because of their attitude, not because of their aptitude.
I also suggest that almost all the obstacles which limit our effectiveness as classroom behaviour managers are either emotional or mental obstacles. Nervousness, self-doubt, self-recrimination, poor motivation

or self-discipline and lack of enthusiasm account for nearly all the obstacles which limit our effectiveness in the classroom.

I remember walking down a busy street in Liverpool on a crisp autumn morning, next to a small boy and his dad. The father pointed to a shiny green sports car parked on the side of the street and said, *What's that, son?* The little boy looked up to his dad and replied, *Foreign crap, dad.* With a gentle tousle of the boy's hair and a yellowish grin, the father said, *That's right, son,* and hand in hand they continued down the road together.

What that father was doing was helping instil in his son a very definite belief system about a certain type of car- 'foreign cars are crap!' As the youngster grows up his experience with foreign cars will tend to verify his expectations of them. They will truly appear to him to be over priced, less reliable, less attractive and less responsive than the local beauties he will most likely choose to drive. Belief systems, attitudes and expectations shape our perceptions of  cars, both local and foreign, as well as the children in our classrooms.

At the beginning of the book we  looked at how effective teachers have adopted the belief system that 'Difficult doesn't mean impossible'. This belief system shapes their perception of  every event that takes place in their classrooms. With this belief system, highly effective teachers are

**...keep coming back with enough energy and enthusiasm to try again where others before them have failed.**

able to persevere when faced with challenging behaviour. They keep coming back with enough energy and enthusiasm to try again where others before them have failed.

Further, we examined how highly effective behaviour managers don't have this empowering belief system through the use of will power alone or because they try harder. Their empowering belief system emerges in response to many assumptions they make about behaviour. Imagine their belief system as a tabletop. The only way the tabletop can stand is as a result of the four legs that support it. The four major legs that support the belief system that 'Difficult doesn't mean impossible' are the assumptions that:

- behaviour is learned and new behaviours can be learned;
- behaviour is effective. It's getting needs met, otherwise it wouldn't exist;
- it's not what the behaviour looks like that's important but what the behaviour is trying to tell you; and
- behaviour exists as part of a system and responds to all other parts of the system.

These assumptions, and the belief system they support, form the core, the hidden power behind effective behaviour management in the classroom. From this core emerges what I call a 'choice-driven' approach to teaching. Highly effective teachers are 'choice-driven'. They deliberately choose:

- their own focus. They use the 'greens and the sandtraps' strategy to look for what it is that they hope to find - appropriate behaviour;
- to use a model of influence, not control. Highly effective teachers understand that control is an illusion;
- to accept responsibility for their own emotional wellbeing;
- to take responsibility for their part in keeping the class in the 'temperate zone' by using the 'big toe first' strategy;
- to plan;
- to nurture their classes' 'emotional gardens';
- to provide pay-offs for appropriate behaviour; and
- to focus on the processes, not the product.

**'Choice-driven' teachers are human beings who make blunders just like the rest of us.**

'Choice-driven' teachers are human beings who make blunders just like the rest of us. But they are forgiving of themselves and they have a genuine positive expectancy about the effectiveness of the processes outlined in this book.

Highly effective teachers expect the best from themselves and they very often get it.

I encourage you to use this book to help you find the best within yourself. After all, it's not that hard to find - is it?

# Suggested Reading

- Balson, M. 1984, *Understanding Classroom Behaviour,* ACER, Victoria, Australia.

- Barnhart, D., Charles, C. and Samples, B. 1977, *The Whole School Book,* Addison Wesley, Philippines.

- Brammer, L.M. 1985, *The Helping Relationship,* Prentice Hall Inc., New Jersey.

- Buzan, T. and Gelb, M.J. 1995, *Lessons from the Art of Juggling,* Aurum Press, Harmony Books, Great Britain.

- Dreikurs, R. 1964, *Happy Children,* Fontana/Collins, Glasgow.

- Fiore, Q. and McLuhan, M. 1967, *The Medium is Massage,* Bantam Books, New York.

- Glasser, W. 1975, *Reality Therapy,* Harper and Row, New York.

- Postman, N. and Weingartner, C. 1971, *Teaching As a Subversive Activity,* Penguin Education Specials, Great Britain.

- Reismer, E. 1971, *School is Dead,* Penguin Education Specials, Great Britain.

- Waldrop, M.M. 1992, *Complexity,* Simon and Schuster, New York.